SELLING YOUR FILM

Other Books by Eric Sherman:

THE DIRECTOR'S EVENT (Atheneum 1969)

FRAME BY FRAME: A Handbook for
Creative Filmmaking (Acrobat 1987)

DIRECTING THE FILM: Film Directors
on Their Art (Acrobat 1988)

SELLING YOUR FILM

A GUIDE TO THE CONTEMPORARY MARKETPLACE

Eric Sherman

ACROBAT BOOKS • LOS ANGELES

ISBN#: 0-918226-27-9

Library of Congress Catalog Card Number: 90-081312

Typesetting: Rigney Enterprises

First printing: May 1990

Cover Design: P*h*.D

Acrobat Books
P.O. Box 870
Venice, CA 90294

For information on Eric Sherman film seminars, contact:
    Film Transform, Inc.
    3755 Cahuenga Blvd. West
    Studio City, CA 91604
    818-769-3010

Printed in the United States of America

everal individuals were instrumental in the creation of SELLING YOUR FILM. My publisher Tony Cohan inspired me to put my information about the film industry into book form. He is the quintissential publisher who perceives a market need, then ever so gently creates an environment in which a book *will be written*. I thank him for his confidence in me, and for his conviction that interested readers have the right to know more about subjects that inspire and excite them.

Richard di Giovanni and Jim Long gave lectures on the industry at our film seminars coordinated by Genie Dillard. The response to these lectures demonstrated that most filmmakers are unaware of many of the particulars of the business side of things, but *are* aware of the vital need to learn them. An additional thank you to Genie for continuing to provide the forum where the ideas and concepts, as well as the nuts and bolts, of filmmaking can be aired.

My attorney, Roger Sherman, gave me my first, and still most important, basic rule of the film business—THERE IS NO SUCH THING AS A STANDARD DEAL! He has stood by me throughout my career, motivated by the conviction that if honesty and frankness prevail, then everybody wins.

Peter Dekom, one of the most successful attorneys in Hollywood, has demonstrated that, at all levels of a business, one can still care about the health and sanity of its practitioners. His writings on the enterprise of film, if collected, would provide a primer for anyone interested in diving into this game.

L. Ron Hubbard, whose management technology allowed me to organize these principles, has provided me with a sane outlook in a world that uneasily mixes art and commerce.

To everyone mentioned above, and to my students, who keep listening, THANK YOU!

TABLE OF CONTENTS

FOREWORD

A recent survey of the leading U.S. booksellers of film- and video-related titles revealed that the most urgently needed information was about the *business* of film.

There are several reasons why there is so little material available on this subject, as compared with the art, craft and history of the medium.

First, the business changes continuously. Last year's stable operating rules, even last month's, might be radically different today. The film industry and its codes of practice—written and unwritten—have been evolving steadily ever since the Paramount Consent Decree of the late 40's and early 50's. In fact, no changes so large have occurred since the Sony buyout of Columbia and the Time-Warner merger at the end of the 80's.

So any serious student of the industry must stay sensitive and open at all times, lest he be stuck with fixed ideas which will cripple his ability to survive, let alone flourish. Even Peter Dekom, one of the most prominent entertainment attorneys in Hollywood and an avid student of the industry, has avoided collecting his excellent articles and other writings into a book out of concern over the currency of the information.

Second, those individuals who *do* have an understanding of the game are often reluctant to part with their secrets. In a game in

ix

which so many desire to play and so few apparently prevail, there is a fear that if the next person finds out the rules, then one's own position may be jeopardized. This fear is probably irrational, since a serious investigation of the ups and downs of the business reveals that, ultimately, creative talent wins out and that persistence, not insider information, is the telling variable in determining one's success.

If one considers management vs. talent as "the art of power" vs. "the power of art," one quickly sees that although it is glamorous, intriguing and "sexy" to see the film business as money- or power-driven, in fact it has always been driven by creative talent. The filmmaker continually has to remind himself of that.

Thirdly, the laws and codes of practice governing the film and other media industries have been changing so rapidly and growing so complex that people on the outside see it as an unfathomable jungle, and people on the inside rarely can get enough breathing room to gain a perspective on the implications of new developments enough to pass it on to others.

Finally, the explosion of technological advances (video in all its forms and formats, cable, satellite, High Definition Television [HDTV], etc.) has had a wide-reaching effect on the business life and potential of a film or video product.

Whereas a film used to have one chance in ten of recouping its cost, and had a shelf-life of three months or so in theatres, we are now approaching a 50-50 chance for recoupment in films of certain genres and budget levels, and a shelf-life via the ancillary (foreign, video, cable, etc.) markets of 18 months or more. Keeping track of how these technological changes alter business considerations is formidable, and very few people are current in all domains.

Nonetheless, it *is* possible to extract some basic guidelines and rules that have been true throughout the past few decades, and any filmmaker who wishes to survive must learn these laws—and then choose whether to follow or change them.

INTRODUCTION

For someone who wishes to make films, I had something of an ideal background. I grew up in Hollywood (actually Van Nuys, when it was all orange ranches); had a father who was an active and well-respected director (Vincent Sherman); spent many Saturdays watching movies being made at Warner Bros. (when they had a normal six-day work week); and had many a lunch in the executive dining room (which seemed quite normal to me).

I went to college in the mid-60's, when aside from USC, UCLA and NYU, almost nobody dared "study" film. You could study theater, literature, painting, or any of the classical arts, but working on film was strictly a "guerilla" activity. At Yale, where I was a math major, we had the Yale Film Society, one of the first and eventually the largest college groups dedicated to showing "auteurist" works (films directed by individuals with strong visual styles and identifiable themes).

We hired Andrew Sarris, then film critic of *The Village Voice*, to give a presentation on the artistic merit of Samuel Fuller's "Shock Corridor." This, I believe, was one of the first times a critic was actually paid to talk about a film!

Though my familial background would have seemed to set me up for filmmaking, and though my father seemed to lead an interesting and exciting life, I was not aware of any personal attraction to the production side of the medium. I was content to be on the "leading edge" of film appreciation.

But my associates at the Yale Film Society were determined to carry our maverick approach beyond the aesthete level all the way through to production. There were no film courses, so we begged, borrowed and rented equipment, instruction manuals, old black and white film, and a set of lights. We proceeded to make a number of movies, several of which ended up being shown at major international film festivals and being excellently reviewed by *Variety* and other trade magazines.

We were the classic example of people who didn't know that we couldn't do it...so we did it!

As a junior, I and a Film Society colleague, Martin Rubin, wrote what turned out to be one of the first books in the English language on American film directors, *The Director's Event* (Atheneum, 1969). We did this mostly as an excuse to meet some of the people we had most come to revere as artists.

To graduate in the Scholar of the House program, I made a documentary film on the great saxaphonist Charles Lloyd, which *Variety* called "perhaps the best film ever made on a jazz musician." Independent distributors from around the country contacted me. I sold or leased the film to a number of colleges, libraries and "midnight specials."

Then I went back to L.A. and waited for my phone to ring. It didn't.

I couldn't understand how all these credentials—bloodline, Yale degree, book, notable documentary—did not add up to a blossoming film career.

I pursued my writing and documentary work, and then was asked by the American Film Institute in 1976 to cull all their 10,000 pages of interviews with directors and create *the* book on film directing. Another writer had been assigned the task previously but had, according to reports, fled the project when he learned that no two of the 80-plus directors interviewed agreed on even the most fundamental aspect of what constituted his work.

Having been raised around the studios and having come to know many directors, including my father, the above fact seemed to me the key. The startlingly simple truth was, indeed, that no two directors agreed about the solutions to the problems of their craft and art. In fact, they did not even agree on a definition of what a film director was!

However, they did virtually all agree as to what these problems were. The book that resulted, *Directing The Film* (Little, Brown, 1976; re-released by Acrobat, 1988) became a problem-identifying and problem-solving manual that is still read today as a primer on directing.

But an area given perhaps least attention by these filmmakers interviewed for *Directing The Film* was the *business* side of things. Few of them had the entrepreneurial bent of so many of today's directors. Few had ever financed their own pictures, let alone negotiated distribution deals or haggled over "world-wide ancillary rights." The majority of them, even the successful producer-directors, such as Howard Hawks, had developed their careers firmly in the Hollywood major studio tradition. They were expected to make good commercially acceptable pictures; that was all.

In the post-Vietnam war era, with exponentially rising production costs, the explosion of new and lucrative markets for film product on a world-wide multi-media basis, and the growing supremacy of "the deal" vs. the picture, very few of the classic directors would have known how to grapple with the new set of problems facing the industry.

The 70's and 80's produced a climate for filmmakers where learning the craft was but one of the hurdles to overcome. Mastering the business, or surrounding oneself with a team of lawyers, agents and other representatives who had, became no longer a luxury or well-advised, it became a necessity for mere survival, let alone expansion.

I now understand why my phone had failed to ring upon my return to Los Angeles in 1970. While I had paid some dues craft-wise and art-wise, I was naive regarding business affairs. I had no knowledge or understanding of marketing, public relations, deal-making, financing, contract law, and so on. My knowledge of filmmaking had been limited entirely to part of Phase One of a three-phase enterprise. I knew hard-core production, but the worlds of distribution, exhibition, and the business codes and practices of all three phases were mysteries, "best left to the experts."

Furthermore, though I *knew* I didn't know those areas (which put me a step ahead of several of my colleagues), I *feared* knowing them. I had fallen into the time-honored tradition that an artist (which I had hoped I was), once tainted with knowledge of money and related matters, would somehow forever lose, or at least compromise, his art. The simple insight I had failed to gain, though, was that if an artist doesn't didn't know the rules of his game, he can easily be exploited.

The problem for the artist, then, is how to gain knowledge of the business normally left to the "experts," without forgetting that it is the result of his creative work that allows the experts to have a playing field. The difficulty for the artist with learning "deal-making" is that it is apparently so complex that he may forget it is his art that got him there in the first place.

Any specialized field of knowledge contains this danger: when one becomes immersed in it, he can forget the simplicities from which the complexities stemmed. This is the theme and organizing principle driving this book—to lay out as simply as possible the fundamentals of the film business, from the perspective not of an attorney or business affairs expert, but the creator of film products and sub-products. Wherever possible and appropriate, I will tie the business and economic truths back to the work of the filmmaker, without whose efforts there would be no film "business."

Except perhaps for the independently wealthy, today's "compleat filmmaker" absolutely must gain a working knowledge of the ever-widening scope and impact of his work in the market, if he wishes to create the effects he set out to achieve at the beginning.

FILM—THE TRIPLE-TIERED INDUSTRY

F or filmmakers, the name of the game is production. All their hopes, dreams, and efforts are involved with it. All their satisfactions and frustrations are tied in with it. But production is but one level of the industry. It is the one which most concerns filmmakers, but not the sole determinant of a film's fate. Perhaps because of this, you will hear people in the industry say, "you can't tell what an audience will like." This is a dangerous assumption, leading to unpredictable results and an apparently random selection of "go," or "greenlighted," projects in the first place.

The result of production is *completed films*. But a completed film has no value if not seen seen by people. These opportunities

3

are created by *distributors* and *exhibitors*. So he who considers it's "up to the fates" whether or not his film is a success, assumes that his responsibility starts and stops with the act of production. It is almost as if he considers that distribution and exhibition are a matter of the audiences' whim, so he sees his film this way. But abundant data now exists indicating that distribution and exhibition, like production, can be created and controlled to yield far more predictable results than ever before. While there are factors which increase or decrease the filmmaker's degree of control, a knowledge of the basics enables him to deal effectively with these determining factors in his projects, and in his career.

BEGINNINGS

It can be argued that the film industry actually grew up backwards from the way it is usually portrayed. Entrepreneurs who owned exhibition venues (saloons, early theatres, etc.) needed showable product to project on the often makeshift screens in their facilities. They established teams to grind out as much product as possible, given time (availability of sunlight) and economic restraints. The one- and two-reel (10- and 20- minute) short films that dominated the early days of the industry were greedily consumed by audiences who always seemed to want more. As the land and theatre holdings and demand for product grew, the owners had not only to find newer, more cost-effective and quicker ways to produce and show films, they had to find ways to distribute them across their network of theaters.

Thus, the triad of *production-distribution-exhibition* grew organically, each needing the other two to function smoothly and profitably. And things did progress relatively smoothly until two key events occurred: the advent of television and its attendant need for outside financing for the vast amount of product suddenly needed to fill the airwaves; and the disgruntlement of some independent producers who allegedly could not get their motion pictures shown at theatres owned by the major producers and distributors. The former resulted in the beginning of "bottom-line dominated" producing, and the latter in the legal manifesto known as the Paramount Consent Decree.

Certainly filmmaking had always paid due attention to the bottom-line, or costs and potential profits, but as most of the survivors of the mogul-dominated era recall, the moguls were, if not filmmakers themselves, at least showmen who had a love for their product. Decisions on "go" pictures would be made at least in part by the instincts and hunches of the studio heads, rather than the dictates of bankers, boards of directors, or the power-cluster agents who appeared to rule the late 80's. (I do not think it is to over-idealize or romanticize the Golden Age of Hollywood to say that at least the staff writers, producers and directors felt they were making their pictures for people who, profit or loss, had some appreciation of the work that went into them. Many active filmmakers of today state that they feel they're making their pictures for a faceless board of directors whose *only* consideration is the picture's contribution to the profit-loss statement. They hope and pray that by the time their film is released, it bears some resemblance to their original intention and will find an audience somewhere.)

THE CONSENT DECREE

The Paramount Consent Decree (which, by the way, has been tested during the Reagan era and can safely be said to be in a state of interpretive flux) is one of those historical shifts which purportedly attempted to increase fairness in the competitive marketplace for screen space and time. In fact, it ended up so aberrating the relations among filmmakers, distributors and exhibitors that many of today's common industry practices—which fill the studios with reams of convoluted contracts between talent and management, and between producer and distributor, and fill the courts with lawsuits—actually were born out of fears generated by the decree. (I have seen the definition of "net profit" by one major studio in their "standard contract." It is 12 legal-sized, single-spaced pages!) Whereas prior to the decree it may have been difficult for independents to compete with the majors due to lack of available screens for their product, after the decree, both sides of the equation (producers and distributors on one side, exhibitors on the other) resorted to freaky and often illegal methods to control the other.

In keeping with the theme of the Sherman and Clayton Anti-Trust Acts, which limited the control of an end-product by its originators, the Consent Decree essentially stated that a single entity could not produce, distribute, and exhibit a product. This was thought to constitute a monopoly of sorts which would prohibit independently-made product from exposure to the public, and thus a fair shake at profits. The major studios opted to "consent" to this legal opinion and divest themselves of their theatres, avoiding protracted and expensive lawsuits (at least until the dubious testing of these limits through major stock purchases by the studios into exhibition chains during the late 80's). The fact that there were still theatres known as "Paramount," "Warners," "Loews," "Fox," etc., did not indicate any formal relationship between supplier of product and seller to the public. But instead of this opening the exhibitors' doors to independent product, it brought about a number of unusual solutions to deal with this artificially created problem. Unfortunately, it is the haggling over the resolution to these problems that seems to dominate the marketplace today, not a wide-open marketplace for deserving films. Because these wars are being fought, every educated film-maker should be aware of the factors driving each side. While not every filmmaker needs to or should play this game, unawareness of it constitutes a deliberate blind-sidedness which can only limit his understanding and ultimately his effectiveness in getting his films made and shown.

6

BOOK ONE

PRODUCTION

PRODUCTION

Definition: *the ideas and activities (including all the work of screenwriting, acting, cinematography, editing, directing and associated creative and administrative fields including finance) which constitute the enterprise of film- or video-making.*

Result: *a completed motion picture or video, suitable for selling to an audience that wants to see it.*

CHAPTER 1

ACQUIRING THE PROPERTY

I n most film courses, the focus is on film or video production, how best to get a creative idea from the mind onto the screen, how the tools of the craft can best be utilized by the artist to translate the creative impulse into concrete form.

9

But over the past decade, there has been more and more interest in questions that are essentially administrative or financial. As the film industry has veered more and more toward the extremes of megalithic production-distribution entities on one side, and encampments of modest creative entrepreneurs on the other, individual game players have been on the search for stable rules and guidelines they can follow in making career, or at least project, choices.

There used to be a strong middle ground of producer-distributor groups, known as the *mini-majors*. For a while, the independent filmmaking community felt that these companies represented a new resource for more individualistic projects. But as Thomas Pryor noted not insignificantly in his 80's wrap-up for *Daily Variety* (28 December, 1989 issue), "Of course, it was not so long ago when mini-majors were evolving all over the place. But where are they now—gone with the wind!"

The usual production cycle goes like this:

An individual gets an idea for a movie or video. This idea comes from the creative imagination, or is suggested by a book, newspaper article, poem, a work in another artistic medium, or even by another movie.

The person writes it down in the form of an *outline*; a *treatment* (a short prose summary of the events and characters of a film). Length is anywhere from one to 30 pages, with an average of about 10. No set format); or a *screenplay* (a technical written format including a description of the events—providing narrative thrust—and the dialogue—providing the sense of character—that serves as the backbone of a film. Current industry practice is *not* to include camera shots at this selling stage of a screenplay. Length is usually 90–120 pages. Agreed-upon format is peculiar to each country.)

While he might at this point endeavor to finance the production, it is more common today for him to seek other creative elements to associate with the script before he attempts to market it.

These elements might include known talent, such as actors or a director. (If he groups enough of these elements together, he is now marketing a "package" more than a script.) The advantage to this method of packaging is that it could appear to potential sources of financing to be a more commercially assured venture, especially if the actors or director had themselves ever been associated with a successful picture.

The theory here, of course, is that if the written screenplay is alone substantial enough to gain the commitment of other established film business entities, then that is a vote of confidence for the material. The potential disadvantage to the package is that the finance source might consider the included extra talent to be an encumbrance rather than an asset, limiting the future selling rather than enhancing it.

PROTECTING YOUR RIGHTS

Before we go further into financing techniques, there are a number of important guidelines to be followed by the entrepreneurial writer in preparing his project for market.

First and foremost is establishing the ownership of the written material. This is usually done by one or more of three methods: (1) gaining a copyright from the Library of Congress, Copyright Office in Washington, D.C.; (2) registering the material with the Writers Guild of America, West; (3) mailing a copy of the screenplay to oneself, registered or certified, return receipt requested, and then storing it sealed until it may be needed for legal demonstration.

To copyright a written work is a very simple procedure. In essence, one types "Copyright 199_ by Author's Name" on the cover sheet. That alone is protective. A complete filing involves calling or writing the Copyright Office in D.C. and requesting literary copyright forms. One then fills it out with the requested number of copies of the screenplay and/or treatment enclosed

11

and sends it back with a nominal fee. The Copyright Office sends you certification.

Copyright law is complex, and if there is any question as to whether or not another individual or group has a stake in the copyright, one really should employ an excellent copyright attorney, who can be recommended by fellow filmmakers or local Bar Associations. As to what rights and privileges you actually gain by holding the copyright to a work, you will need professional legal advice.

The protection offered by the Writers Guild of America, West, Script Registration Division (Hollywood, CA), is also excellent, and is a service offered to any writer, not just a member of the Guild. Ideally, one takes a copy of the script to the Script Registration Office, fills out a form, pays a fee, and the Guild seals away a copy of your script. More than protecting the written content, this procedure establishes the date at which you completed your work. This date could become a key factor later if another author or producer claims to have generated a similar work. The Guild will accept any number of treatments or drafts of the screenplay, so it's a good idea to keep registering new drafts as long as there are significant changes.

When you complete the registration process, the Guild gives you a certificate with a number on it. It is common for writers to type this number onto the title page of their screenplay: "Registered WGAW # ____."

A title alone without a manuscript cannot be registered through the Writers Guild. There is a title registration service offered as a privilege to members of the MPPA (Motion Picture Producers' Association, headquartered in New York).

While there may be some legal value to sending a copy of your script to yourself through the mails and keeping it sealed, I would recommend the above two methods, Copyright and WGAW Registration. They are more professional and allow you to write those protection notices on the script itself. Then the reader knows you've taken enough care with your work to fully secure right of ownership.

As for actual ownership, an author will be expected to be responsible for asserting that he, in fact, does own the material he's selling. In other words, if he is fortunate enough to find financing for his project from a producer, distributor or any other source, that source will, or should, ask the writer to warrant that he has the rights to make the sale.

The writer will probably be asked to indemnify the funding source against claims of ownership from other parties. For example, if the writer dreamed up his script idea based on a friend's suggestion, or even based on casual conversations with a friend, the writer would be well-advised, prior to selling the script, to secure from the friend a simple statement vesting full ownership of the material with the screenplay's author.

If the friend and the author wish to have some agreed-upon compensation under certain future circumstances, then this should be stated in their agreement. So the author should remember that no financier of a picture will want to purchase any property where the prior rights of ownership are in any way unclear or unresolved.

Your pal, with whom you dreamed up the concept, should be willing to help you get yourself in the legally acceptable position of representing full ownership rights. If he says, "Oh, don't worry about it. We'll work it out if something comes of it," this is an invitation to disaster. His unwillingness to confront with you, there and then, what he would consider to be fair treatment should you have success, breeds an air of uncertainty which can haunt a project. I've seen many friendships dissolve over just such disputes.

Now if you are not yourself a writer, but you find written material or commission someone to generate material for you, then you are serving, at least at this stage, as a *producer* (one who guides a film or video project through administrative and creative

13

barriers to its completion as a film or video suitable for distribution and exhibition).

Your goal, no doubt, will be to identify funding for the production, obtain it, and get the picture made. Just as the writer will have to grant to you the necessary ownership for you to take it to market, you in turn will have to warrant to the financier that you have these rights, and you will be granting to the funder at least some of these rights in exchange for the money to make the project.

ACQUIRING RIGHTS

As a producer, there are a number of ways you can acquire the rights to the written material.

First, you can buy it outright from the commissioned author. With a simple contract, you agree to exchange X dollars for a service rendered. You would state to the hired author that these X dollars buy all rights to this material in this or any other form now contemplated or which may appear in the future. You will specify that the author does not retain any rights of ownership to the material, either explicit or implicit, except as stated in the contract.

Such a business agreement should be negotiated and drawn up with the advice of a qualified attorney. You might even be well-advised to suggest to the author that if he has any question over the propriety of this arrangement that he should consult an attorney of his own. You would not ever want it stated that he signed this agreement under duress.

If the author happens to be a member of the Writers Guild of America, then (a) you would have to meet certain minimum terms as described by the Writers Guild guidelines for the genre of the material being written, and (b) you yourself would have to be a signatory to the basic Writers Guild agreement. There is some cost associated with this, but it is basically for everyone's protection. (It is also a cost that could be reimbursed out of production funds at a later date, but this would need to be disclosed while making the financing arrangement.)

OPTIONS

Another choice for the producer is to *option* the screenplay that he has found or commissioned to be written. An option is an agreement between a writer and a future buyer of the written material. The agreement usually spells out:

(a) an amount of money or other consideration to be paid for the option

(b) when exactly the option starts, and what amount of time the option lasts

(c) the amount of money the prospective buyer will pay to the writer prior to expiration of the option should the buyer decide to purchase the screenplay

(d) who, if anyone, has the rights to extend the length of time of the option (is it unilateral, or by joint agreement?)

(e) what funds will change hands if the option is extended

(f) if the screenplay is purchased, was it an advance against the future purchase price, or was it a separate fee?

(g) what is the status of the option monies if the buyer does not exercise the purchasing rights (does the writer keep the money *and* the full rights to the screenplay? does the writer have to return any of the money to the erstwhile purchaser if the writer should sell the material to someone else at a later date? etc.)

(h) are there any other considerations associated with the option (is the producer or purchaser required to employ the writer of this draft of the screenplay on future drafts? or to use his best efforts to do so? or is no such arrangement implied?)

The Writers Guild issues guidelines on the minimum amounts for these rights, and these must be followed if the writer is a member. The Writers Guild also will provide a standard or model option form upon request. As with most other paper forms associated with film production, samples and models can be acquired from Enterprise Stationers, 7401 Sunset Blvd., Los Angeles, CA 90046.

PURCHASE

If there is no option agreement, or if the option to purchase is exercised, then we move into an outright "literary purchase agreement." It is equally important in this case to enumerate any and all rights, stated or implied. For example:

(a) has the buyer purchased the rights to make one motion picture from this material, or any number of motion pictures?

(b) if rights to sequels are included, is there to be additional pay or other considerations?

(c) similar points to (a) and (b) regarding television movies-of-the-week, mini-series, series, novelization, videotapes, radio, theatrical play or musicalization, and all other ancillary rights (comic books or strips, posters, other promotional items, etc.)

(d) in whose name will the copyrights for all these works be filed?

Many legal authorities recommend that you keep notes on every phone call, creative meeting or business meeting that you have regarding your film project. Sometimes it's even advisable to send a letter (and, of course, keep a copy for yourself) to the other people who participated in the meeting, summarizing your understanding of what occurred, and stating that if their understanding is different, you will expect them to communicate such to you.

The purpose of all the above is certainly not to frighten you or make you overly suspicious of the people with whom you're attempting to do business. But the complexity of these matters is testimony to the high value placed on screenwriting and the attendant rights to its results. One would like to think that if someone values your work enough to steal it, they'd hire you in the first place (saves a lot of time and bother, and after all, you were the source of it), but this isn't always the case.

But a number of recent lawsuits have demonstrated (most notably, the Art Buchwald vs. Paramount case) that there doesn't necessarily even need to be intentional theft. An idea suggested at some story conference may, years later, emerge in another project altogether, and anyone associated with the creation of that idea may be ruled to have a stake in its success.

For this reason, many potential funding sources (producers, major studios, independents, distributors), and even literary agents, will not even read "unsolicited" material for fear that you will one day have a future claim against them.

The two common solutions to this are: (1) if you are submitting material yourself to a funding source, and if you are willing to take the associated risks, state your willingness to sign a "Release," in essence quitting any future claim you may have should you decide your work was plagiarized; (2) submit your work via an entity known to the funding source, such as a literary or other talent agent used to dealing with film groups.

So considering all the above, unless you are planning to wear all the hats connected with the realization of your film project —producer, writer, financier, etc.,—your best bet is to leave a rational paper trail showing each step of your progress so it can be retraced if needed.

CHAPTER 2

FINANCING YOUR FILM OR VIDEO

O f all the arts, film and architecture are the most driven by economics. Because their creations are so expensive to produce, it sometimes appears as if these arts are *only* economics-driven. But the remarkable escalation in major studio production costs, from an average of $400-500 thousand in the 1940's to close to $20 million by the end of the 80's, far outstrips U.S. inflation rates.

On analysis, the reasons for this have as much to do with the attempt to control product in the marketplace (if films cost $20 million to make, then only big companies can make them), and with producers and studios locking in giant fees and overheads for themselves (instead of waiting to determine the success of the picture), as with any fundamental production reason.

So in considering finance sources for your project, it's a good idea to recognize that the major studio route is but one, and has a relatively low probability of success at that. Then proceed to learn the realities of your particular budget needs.

GOALS OF FINANCIERS

In essence, regardless of your finance source, you are seeking investors who have reason to believe in the quality and commercial viability of your project.

There are certain elements common to all investments:
1. Preservation of capital
2. Potential for growth of capital
3. Income
4. Tax benefits
5. Pride of ownership (and other emotional factors)

Let's take a look now at how each of these finance goals ties in with film investments.

1. **Preservation of capital**. The classic "safe" investments—developed real estate, savings bonds, municipal bonds, Treasury bills—achieved their status by offering the investor something tangible in exchange for his money. An investment backed by the treasury of a government or by the ultimately limited amount of land and the perennial need for housing seems to be a good bet.

The usual assumption is: "there's only so low these can go," or "people will always need housing," or "this investment is safe unless the U.S. government goes under...and if that happens, nothing has value anyway."

Movies are generally considered to be a poor investment from this viewpoint. Unless you pre-sell your movie in enough markets to garner a "guaranteed" advance equal to or greater than the production costs, then there is no preservation of capital associated with a film. And if you do pre-sell the movie to that extent,

19

the chances are that the total guaranteed advance is all that you will ever see, even if the film becomes more profitable later on.

Furthermore, the "guarantor" usually retains enough provisions for escape clauses (if the movie is not up to some "professional" standard, or is deemed not to deliver what was promised in the script) that his guarantee isn't all that certain anyway.

Moreover, if you manage to retain some rights while selling off others in the hopes to get at least some guaranteed return, then the value of the retained rights becomes gradually less because a future buyer of the remaining rights will not have the "plum" rights (U.S. and foreign video) to back up his investment.

So except in certain specific circumstances, pre-sells have as many liabilities as potential benefits.

Is there *any* way to preserve capital in a movie investment? In the answer to this question lies the genesis, I believe, of the star system.

The presence of a bona fide movie star who has previously appeared in a money-making film may be sufficient lure in a pre-sell not just to get a guarantee, but a "non-returnable cash guarantee" in advance from a distributor or exhibitor. So it is considered that some movie investors would rather spend several million dollars more than the actual production cost of the picture in order to lock in a star's participation, anticipating that this would more than pay for itself in cash commitments from future consumers of the product.

There are no reliable statistics on this point, but it's a fair guess that it has failed to pay off at least as often or more often than it has succeeded. There are many examples, in fact, of films with no stars whatsoever being the most successful pictures of their year, especially when measured against production costs (*American Graffiti; sex, lies and videotape*).

But overall, films do not hold up as an assured method of preserving capital.

2. **Potential for growth of capital.** Whereas a wise investor

might buy a stock in a new company in hopes that it will become the next Polaroid, Xerox or IBM, or buy a piece of undeveloped land in an area he hopes will become the next Malibu or Beverly Hills, there are only a few such instances where he would invest in a movie.

Occasionally, one hears of a genre film (horror, farce, etc.) produced privately at a very low cost and the producers turned around and created a bidding war among distributors, receiving a cash advance or buyout at many times the original investment. This is the exception rather than the rule, and should never be counted upon or anticipated.

It takes a rare combination of circumstances, along with excellent public relations skills and unusually high business acumen, to pull this off.

Another possible way a movie investment could bring a high return to an investor is by becoming so phenomenally successful in several markets (theatrical, video, etc.) that even with considering the "creative" bookkeeping practices commonly alleged in the film industry, the distributor is forced to return profits to the producer. Again, this is not to be counted upon, especially among those just starting out in the industry.

3. **Income.** Since most films do not pay out profits, if any, for at least the first year to year-and-a-half of a picture's release—and then usually only at six month intervals—regular income is not a strong lure to invest in a film. For this reason, income-oriented investors might prefer to invest in a major film company's stock or bonds, especially if they pay quarterly dividends.

Some finance groups are experimenting with innovative film investment products, such as buying into a film *and* a security (insurance policy or other annuity, "zero-coupon bond," etc.), and having the security pay out regularly while they're awaiting the film's hoped-for profits. It is too early to tell if any of these will meet their projected returns to investors.

4. **Tax benefits.** Prior to the Tax Reform Acts of 1976 and

21

1986, there were some tax benefits associated with film investing in the U.S. Most of those have vanished. In some cases, depreciations (writing off a portion of a film's perceived loss in value over time) are possible. In other cases, if the film is a "passive investment" (the investor does not actively work on the picture in a production or consulting capacity), there can be passive losses which could offset some passive gains in other parts of the investor's portfolio.

But at this time, tax benefits are not a compelling reason to invest in film.

In some countries, advertising and promotional dollars are given a considerable tax advantage, and some U.S. finance groups have explored "P&A Funds" (funds of money earmarked not for production, but for copies or prints of the film and advertising for the film), testing the waters to see if the I.R.S. will extend any benefits to them.

The entire question of film investments and tax advantages is complex, as are most issues associated with the I.R.S., and you should consult a qualified tax advisor or attorney, and counsel your investors to do the same regarding any financial involvement with a film project.

5. **Pride of ownership (and other emotional factors).** This is probably the best reason of all for someone to invest money in a film. As with oil wells, race horses and fine art, there is a tremendous emotional charge associated with movies for many investors. Since the explosion of ancillary markets (additional outlets for film beyond U.S. theaters, such as video, foreign, etc.) has increased the likelihood that a decently made film will return at least some money on the investment, the emotional reasons for film investment have become more financially justifiable.

Seeing one's name on screen or in advertisements as a Producer or Executive Producer can be well worth the financial risk, especially if it has some public relations value to the investor which he could not otherwise obtain. If the film or video project is on a topic of personal interest to the investor (this becomes especially true with documentaries and made-for-home videos), there is all the more emotional value.

As long as you disclose the financial risk to the investor, it seems to me that personal satisfaction is a strong and justifiable reason for a potential film funder to invest. On top of it, if he gets any of his money back, not to mention profits, you may have a friend for life, if not the start of an investor pool which you can return to for future projects.

One group in New York has built an extremely successful production and distribution company (debt-free, all cash business, wholly owned by them) over the past 15 years with the same group of 10 production investors with whom they started; but where each investor initially put $1,000 in a project, they now each put $100,000 or more into every production.

FUNDING SOURCES

There are numerous potential funding sources for film and video projects, some traditional and some innovative. It is likely that more funding sources and mechanisms will be developed in the future, especially as investment law, tax law, media technology and public interest change. At this time, these are the most common production finance sources for individual filmmaker-entrepreneurs:

1. Major motion picture studios
2. Individual producers with their own funding sources
3. Distributors
4. Banks—
   A. Secured loans
   B. Letters of credit
5. Private investors—
   A. Limited Partnerships
   B. Corporate entities

     C. "Private Placements"

     D. Registered public offerings

  6. Exhibitors.

Let's examine these one at a time and hit some highlights. The following information should not be taken as legal advice. Only a qualified attorney can give you that. However, these are some basic concepts that anyone getting into the area of financing their own projects should know.

MAJOR MOTION PICTURE STUDIOS

Many filmmakers starting out either write a script, or acquire a script (as discussed above). This, called "the property" or "the project," becomes their calling card. The idea is that if they can show it to enough people within major studios, someone will recognize its excellence and option or buy the project and, hopefully, the individual's future services.

It is preferable to take this route via an established attorney or agent who already knows people within the studio and can target the material, for in many cases, unless the writer or option-holder signs a release form, the studio won't even accept the project for review unless it does come from a known entity.

If the release form is signed, or if the agent or attorney sends the material not to any specifically targeted individual within the studio but just as a general mailing, the script will wind up in the Story Department for evaluation.

There, it will be assigned to a "reader" who will synopsize the plot and leading characters on a one-page form, then will recommend that the property be rejected or considered further. These readers are, in some cases, quite skilled and have a keen eye for material that will appeal to the producers, directors and stars who often work with that studio. In other cases, however, the reader may be a very young man or woman, in or just out of college, who is reading these scripts quite quickly for a small fee,

24

and is mostly interested in being seen as astute and talented in the eyes of the department head.

Often the "reader" has come to be a glorified "no-person," because most young, inexperienced readers wouldn't want to risk recommending a project for production that his seniors thought was poor. It is safer to say "no" and impress the boss with his discerning reader's eye.

If by some chance at this stage the script is recommended for further consideration, it will usually pass on to the head of the Story Department, known as the Story Editor. This person is usually an executive at the studio and in constant touch with both the producers who are developing projects there, and the company's "vice-presidents in charge of production," who keep the story editor notified of the kinds of pictures they want to make.

This way, the story editor will know whether or not to pass the script on to a producer, regardless of how well it has been written.

An interesting "whipsaw" that can occur is that a story editor will recognize the excellence of a project, recommend it for production, and a production head will agree. But the genre or style is not something the studio is planning to do in the near future. Still, at that point, they may option the material, in case their production plans change—and so that no one else in Hollywood will make the picture either.

This may not be the conscious purpose behind many studio options, but it has the net effect of "tying up the property" (taking it out of circulation).

It is legendary in Hollywood how many writers have made a decent living from options and renewed options but have never seen one of their scripts made into a movie. While it seems wonderful to get your foot in the door and receive a decent option fee and/or renewal fee, many of these individuals are ultimately quite frustrated and begin to wonder if they are not being used as some kind of a creative pawn in a power game.

For this reason, many writers have opted for the "independent" route where they can be more in charge of their own destiny.

This is a judgment call, and every creative person probably has his own threshold of tolerance for this sort of thing. On the one hand, the amount of money at stake major companies can deliver can be sizable, and can pay the bills for a long time. Also, having *anything* purchased by a major company is a validation of your efforts and lends you a certain credibility, at least for a while.

On the other hand, if too much time passes and your material is only optioned, never produced, your reputation could be tarnished, not to mention the creative frustration of seeing your brainchild never quite materialize.

Therefore, as so often occurs in the film industry, a question of career management crosses over into the creative zone. The answer doesn't always have to be an "either/or." It may be possible to avoid becoming entrapped on either side of this particular game. The answer, of course, is to understand the game first, then choose a path for yourself where you can be in control.

You may need the assistance of an agent or attorney, and certainly you should become familiar with the industry: read the trade magazines, attend seminars, talk with other people who make films or who want to.

Or, you could select other methods of financing!

If you do decide to stick it out in the major studio game, the ideal is this:

1. Your script is read at some level in a studio
2. It is considered worthy of possible production
3. It is routed to an "on-the-lot" producer or production executive who decides to further develop it
4. A fee is paid to you as writer, as writer/producer, or as producer
5. You and/or your writer move on the lot with an office and are given a certain amount of time to rewrite the script according to recommendations from the "supervising" executive or producer

26

6. The rewrite is considered satisfactory and the studio or supervising producer begin the process of interesting a director, stars and other creative talent in participating in your project
7. The "package" is put together with you locked in as co-producer, associate producer, or some equivalent satisfactory (to you and the studio) title. If you are the writer as well, your writing fee and credit are locked in also
8. The picture is produced
9. It is distributed and exhibited publicly, worldwide
10. It meets with critical and audience box-office success, and your future is assured
11. You are offered a deal at the studio to develop additional projects—of your choice or their request. Your agent and/or attorney negotiate a favorable arrangement where everybody wins
12. You continue to generate projects which are produced, and your ability to see your films made grows ever more certain

This is the ideal scene. There are many variations on this, some satisfactory, some dangerous. Your attorney or agent could be your best friend in this case. The key criterion, other than money, is the degree of control you have over the future of your movies.

INDIVIDUAL PRODUCERS WITH THEIR OWN FUNDING SOURCES

Another potential source of funding for your film is an established independent producer who has already set up his own financing —with a studio, a distributor, a bank, a syndicate, etc. The trick is finding the right one.

The first hurdle is knowing which producers have such setups.

Then, you must determine which ones would be most receptive to your project.

You can get a head start on this by having an agent represent you and/or your work. In theory, one of the key benefits of an agent is that he will know who is doing what in the industry, and who needs or is looking for what. This can save a lot of legwork and wasted time waiting for return phone calls.

Or, you can research it yourself by reading the trades and seeing (a) who is announced as having struck what deals where; (b) who has what projects in development or production (by reading the Thursday and Friday production summaries in *Daily Variety* or *The Hollywood Reporter*); and (c) who has produced films over the past few years in a genre similar to yours.

If you do not have ready access to back issues of *Variety* or similar journals, many libraries do. Also, if you live in the Los Angeles area, the library at the Academy of Motion Picture Arts and Sciences in Beverly Hills is open to the public usually four days per week. This is a wonderful institution with extremely gracious and helpful research and reference people. For film students, UCLA, USC and the American Film Institute, as well as universities across the country who have film programs, have excellent research facilities.

Your goal is to determine who are the active producers and, by studying their track record, who is making pictures of the type you admire...or at least can live with.

Some producers will accept "unsolicited" material for review, and some won't. As stated above ("Protecting Your Work"), be prepared to sign a release form, or submit your work via an attorney or agent.

Very few producers will knowingly attempt to steal your ideas. If they are that good, chances are the producer will want to know you and acquire your services along with your existing writing. But aside from the occasional unscrupulous individual or group, it is more likely that if your material has an element of value but is still rejected, the positive parts may unwittingly resurface in a future project by that producer.

In our current litigation-crazed society, and the film industry in particular, many ethical and responsible producers have had to be on their guard against unprofessional writers and promoters who are actually trying to set up a scam situation.

Be marketing-wise. Get the other guy's viewpoint when you are presenting yourself and your project. Be aware of his needs as well as your own, and be prepared to strike a reasonable stance that protects both sides.

One cautionary note: Realize that many established producers have relationships with writers and other talent to whom they wish to filter all their properties for rewrites or additional development. Unless you can demonstrate that your continued participation in the project is to his advantage, or unless your material is so "hot" they simply *must* have you, there is some chance the producer will attempt to buy out your interest in the script.

Again, your best bet is to engage an attorney or agent who will represent your interest. If you have to negotiate a lower price in exchange for some commitment to utilize your services throughout the project, that may ultimately be to your advantage. Remember that you are shaping a career as well as just promoting one movie.

DISTRIBUTORS

Distributors are potential sources of financing for motion picture productions. There are many ways that distributors can lend their considerable clout to your project.

First, under ideal conditions, a distributor may wish to pay directly for your production costs. This is the exception, of course, since unless you are a known entity who has been involved with a previous successful project, they have no way of knowing if you can complete a film, let alone a commercially viable one.

But if you are fortunate enough to create or find story material that is so appealing that a distributor will pay for its realization, then most likely the distributor will end up owning the material outright, or at least will gain long-term exclusive licensing rights to it. This question of ownership has become a highly complex area, and you will definitely need legal assistance in swimming through all the paperwork.

Keep in mind that a distributor will either retain all the rights, world-wide, in all forms of media, or will farm out those rights ("fragmenting") to separate buyers for each medium in each territory of the world. The distributor's primary goal will be to reduce his risk as soon as possible upon involvement with your project. If he didn't do that, he'd not only be liable for the production cost, he'd be losing the interest that his money could have earned sitting in a bank, or invested in a completed film whose quality and commercial potential he could better judge.

Also, remember that not only must the film's production be paid for, someone must pay for the copies of the film that will be shown in theaters and the advertising and promotion that will accompany its release ("Prints and Advertising," or "P&A"). The P&A can equal or surpass the production cost, so this is no small matter.

So it is far more likely that a distributor, if he thinks your project has commercial potential, will offer instead of cash, a "distribution guarantee," or some other form of commitment. If you are resourceful, this commitment can be turned into funding by you with a bank, private investors, or even another production company.

The guarantee, however, will usually contain all sorts of provisos and disclaimers, locking in the distributor's rights to evaluate the film once it's completed and ensure that it is of sufficient quality to be released publicly. No distributor will knowingly show a "turkey," so your financing source must recognize that there is no 100% guarantee from a distributor.

30

Furthermore, the distributor very well knows the value of his written commitment to become involved with your film, so he will often use that to extract more favorable terms than if you had the finished work. (But remember: *THERE IS NO SUCH THING AS A STANDARD DEAL.*) So it would behoove you to package together as many "bankable" elements as possible (director, cast, genre, etc.) before approaching the distributor so as not to be in the position of a beggar.

There are other relationships that can be struck with a distributor. He might give you "an advance against distribution rights." He might be willing to purchase some specific rights, such as a particular medium in a particular geographic region of the world. He might be willing to get involved with a "hot project" if he is also granted exclusive, or "first look," rights to a sequel or to spin-off projects (television series, movies-of-the-week, novelization, etc.).

As with finding the right producer, you must research the world of potential distributors to find out which ones are familiar with your kind of material.

Generally, a distributor whom you are considering approaching as a source of production financing or at least some form of distribution guarantee, will be concerned with these elements of your project: genre, subject matter, script, producer, director, cast, schedule, the existence of a *completion bond* (see section below), whether any other rights have been fragmented or sold off, whether any other source of financing has committed to the project.

In other words, they are looking for a comfort factor. Their commitment to you, at nearly any level, is a bankable commodity. Since their reputation, and ultimately their bankbook, will be on the line, they deserve to be as comfortable with you as you are with them.

As with other sources of financing, you are looking to balance the deck. Some producers who attain funds or commitments from

31

distributors look for the distributor to put at least some money up front. They consider that this will cause the distributor to take a more serious interest in urging the project along.

"How much money?" is a question answerable by examining risks and rewards. Enough to cause their serious interest, but not so much to give them the rights to "buy the farm" cheaply, which could leave you with no viable alternatives to acquire the balance of the funds you'll need.

At this time in the industry, some distributors are leaning toward a willingness to supply the P&A funds if you can get the production financing. This is considered to be a balancing of risks.

The entrepreneurial producer—you—can juggle the players back and forth, extracting more and more certainty of commitment each time, until you finally have everything in place.

The key question, other than selecting the right distributor, is: When in the overall production process should you approach them? Conventional wisdom says that there is an optimum point in the production cycle when a distributor will be most willing to deal with you on favorable terms.

Ideally, you will already be far enough along in your production—you've attained financing from other sources and are well on your way toward actually making the picture—to not require money up front from the distributor, thereby reducing his actual risk. But you are not so far along so as to eliminate the distributor's incentive in getting involved with you.

For this reason, some producers attempt to get at least enough money from private or other sources to shoot some scenes from the picture in order to show the distributor an example of what you have in store. Sometimes pictures start production without complete funding in place for postproduction.

Then the producer will go to the distributor with a rough cut of the picture and attempt to extract completion financing in exchange for limited rights.

If you are very confident in the quality of your project, it could be that you will extract your best deal from a distributor by making the picture entirely on your own (through private financing), then showing him the finished product. If he likes it, you may be able not only to recoup your complete production cost right off the bat, but in fact bargain for a multiple of your costs.

So recoupment isn't your only goal; you might even be able to be in profits right off the bat. Your investors would certainly be happy!

The extreme form of this approach is to not only get your production financed privately, but also to arrive at the distributor with a picture *and* a P&A fund. In that case, you'll probably be able to hire the distributor for a flat fee rather than a fee plus a percentage, because you've reduced the distributor's risk to virtually nothing. This method requires maximum faith from your production investors, but it is probably your most profitable arrangement.

BANKS

Banks have an interesting relationship to film financing. On the one hand, the industry probably wouldn't be here, at least in its present form, without banks' participation. On the other hand, there could hardly be a less likely form of investment for an essentially conservative institution like a bank than film.

The two most common bank interactions with film financing are in the form of *secured loans*, and *letters of credit*.

A secured loan is when the bank holds some kind of concrete asset of yours in exchange for lending you a certain amount of money. If you fail to pay back the money at the agreed-upon time, the bank cashes out the asset and pays off the loan.

In such a transaction, you are hoping that proceeds from selling the film to a distributor, or your share of the box-office returns from the exhibitor via the distributor, will be sufficient to pay back the bank so that you can recover your asset intact. If that asset had originally been borrowed from someone else, you can now return it to the source, along with whatever interest or benefits you had promised the individual. If the asset was your own, then you've produced a picture without cashing out any part of your estate.

Of course, if the proceeds from sale of the film or its box-office performance fail to recoup the amount of the bank loan, the difference has to be made up somehow. Many broken friendships and bankruptcies have occurred in this situation. This leads to a classic dilemma regarding the role of banks in film financing.

By their charter, banks cannot engage in speculative investments risking the capital of their depositors. At the same time, you can argue that if your film is a sure enough bet for someone to stake a significant amount of assets upon in order to secure a bank loan, then why didn't you use the same argument with the source of the assets—get the cash directly—and save everyone the interest payments and paperwork hassle with the bank?

In other words, the very argument that will lead to someone putting up the security for the loan, if it is really strong enough, should be able to cause the cash to be put up, for in either case, if you fail to deliver the expected returns, the source of the asset (or cash) is still out the funds.

Furthermore, remember that a bank will "discount an asset," so you won't get the full value of it in usable production funds. For example, let us say that an investor of yours is willing to put up real estate or bonds as security for the production loan. If the security has an appraised value of $1 million, then it's likely the bank will only lend you somewhere between $800,000 and $900,000. (These discount rates vary widely from bank to bank and change with time.)

So if you can get enough of a performance guarantee from a distributor or exhibitor, it might be best to convert that directly to production cash, if you can, rather than going through the added steps of finding someone with assets who's willing to risk them, discount them, pay interest, conduct the administrative affairs, and so on.

A letter of credit (LC) is where a bank (or another financial institution) extends to you a certain amount of credit. That credit is usually secured by assets you have on deposit with the bank.

Occasionally, if you or your associates have a sizable and substantial enough track record, an LC can be issued on an unsecured basis. But that is by far the exception rather than the rule.

LCs are, themselves, often discounted as well. Some corporations who wish to get involved with films may draw on their existing LCs (secured by their normal operations) to finance their production activities. Of course if they're prudent they never exceed a draw they feel can't be covered by their cash flow from other areas of corporate productivity.

Sometimes one bank or financial institution will issue an LC that another bank or financial institution will then accept as though it were an asset—discount it—and forward the cash for production.

Occasionally, and this is a current area of experimentation in the film community, an entrepreneur will utilize another financial instrument such as an insurance policy, zero coupon bond, or some other reliable form of annuity, and utilize that to secure a loan or LC under the assumption that even if the film fails, the annuity will, in a reasonable amount of time, mature into a value commensurate with the funds borrowed or extended.

If this area interests you, meet with your local bankers and find out their policies regarding film investments. No two banks have identical criteria.

PRIVATE INVESTORS

Private investors, as opposed to financial institutions. make an appealing production funding source to many entrepreneurs.

The contact is individual to individual (in most cases) rather than individual to "faceless" bank. The private investor is an especially ideal source in the case of smaller productions (made-for-home videos, low-budget features, etc.). Since the allure of the movies is so dramatic, sometimes "romantic" individuals will leap at the chance to be involved with pictures.

Prior to the explosion in value of the ancillary markets for film (video cassettes, cable, foreign rights, etc.), only about one out of ten movies made its money back; still, individuals kept investing.

Now, with these additional markets, the right project stands a 50-50 chance or better of recouping its costs and even showing a profit. 50-50 is roughly equivalent to the safest gambling bets (craps, roulette red or black), and that might give you a clue to the demographic profile of the "ideal investor" for film projects—a "high roller" who is aware of the risk, who can afford the loss, and for whom the thrill of the game has a value commensurate with the amount risked.

Unfortunately, unscrupulous entrepreneurs have often failed in the past to disclose fully all the risks associated with such investments, and that has given "production financing" a mixed and sometimes downright dark reputation among potential financiers.

Any producer attempting to raise funds privately should disclose the four major risks associated with film investments:

1. **The film may fail to get completed**. If this happens, of course, the entire enterprise is a loss. Unless the investor had predetermined that he would get some sort of tax or depreciation benefit, then he will suffer the total loss of his funds.

There are two partial protections against this: (a) the incomplete picture could be bought and completed by another production company (though the chances are that this "ambulance chasing" approach will yield far less than the picture would have been worth on the open market if it had been completed by the original production team); (b) a *completion bond* can be secured before the start of production.

A completion bond is an assurance by an outside company (there are half a dozen or so in Hollywood, and numerous others around the world) that the movie's production will be completed.

In order to acquire a bond, the producer, in advance of making the film, submits the script, budget, and list of key production personnel to the bonding company. The company reviews the project and verifies that the picture can be realized for the amount of production funds available to it. The bonding company usually then adds 10% to the budget as a contingency factor, then charges a fee for their bonding services of approximately 6% of the total.

In many cases, the bond company will make an agreement in advance that if the bond is not "invaded" (the bond company does not have to bail out the production with additional funds), they will rebate a portion of their fee (up to half) to the producers.

The benefit of the completion bond is that it provides assurance that the film *will be completed*. Also, for a given production to be "bondable" in the first place is a vote of confidence in the team and the project. And distributors and banks may require that a bond be in place in order for them to become involved in a funding or "guarantee" arrangement.

The liability of a completion bond is that the issuer may reserve the right to alter the script or replace members of the production team if the bonding company representative reports that a picture is going over schedule and/or over budget.

Realistically, the issuer of the bond would rather *not* have to come up with additional production funds in order to finish the film. He *wants* the film to come in on budget, even if certain creative changes have to occur. There can be the mistaken impression that a bond ensures that the film will be *completed at all costs*. The bond actually ensures that the film will be completed on budget, no matter what personnel or creative changes

37

have to occur.

Also, when you receive bonding, you are tacitly agreeing to have a representative or supervisor from the company on the set at all times. This can create significant tension for the production team.

Finally, on a lower budget production, the price of the completion bond might be better spent on the film itself.

If an investor wants some assurance of completion but doesn't want to pay the price of a bond, he always could set aside some funds beyond the film's budget in a bank account with the proviso that this money can only be spent by mutual agreement between the investor and the producer. If the special fund isn't tapped, then it can be returned to the investor upon completion, or could be applied to a P&A fund or to a marketing and promotion campaign.

There is probably a cut-off point in terms of a film's budget, below which a bond is not a wise investment and above which it is an intelligent form of insurance. To know what that point is, you'd need to calculate the cost of each day or week of production, then figure out how many additional days or weeks of filming could be bought with the money otherwise spent on the bond. If it's a week or more, the funds might be better applied to the special production account described above.

In fairness to the major completion bond companies, their staff is usually composed of highly experienced, production-wise people. A responsible bond company can be of substantial help to a film project by identifying potential problem areas.

Many producers have the utmost admiration for the company representatives and consider these individuals not just hatchet people weeding out profligate filmmakers, but supporters of the creative team, even if the film goes somewhat over-budget (within reasonable limits).

The acquisition of a completion bond is a big step in any film production, both for the investors and for the creative team. It should be carefully investigated and considered, taking into account all risks and rewards, before any final decision is made.

Whichever way you go, you should fully disclose to your investors the option of buying the bond, its advantages and liabilities.

2. **The film may be completed but may fail to find a distributor.** As mentioned in an earlier section, the sooner in the filmmaking process you go to a distributor, the more likely it is you'll find one, but the less favorable terms you're likely to get. There is no denying that any potential private investor would be impressed by your legwork and aggressiveness if you secure a distributor in advance of production. He will also take this as a vote of confidence in the project.

However, when the investor finds out what you may have to give away to get this early commitment, he may decide to wait until you at least have some sample film to show.

So the critical issue here is balance. One entertainment attorney who has spent more than 20 years analyzing distribution deals has said that (a) every distribution arrangement is different, and (b) for every production, there is probably an optimum time to seek and lock in a distributor—and this can range from pre-preproduction all the way to after postproduction has been completed.

Questions of genre, cast, delivery time, budget, competition, season of the year, track record of principals and so on all enter into the consideration of when the entrepreneurial producer should seek his distributor relationship. There is a risk-reward balance all the way up and down the line, and each deal should be assessed on its own merits.

3. **The film may find a distributor, but the distributor may fail to gain a satisfactory release schedule or performance guarantee from exhibitors.** In most cases, a distributor won't commit to a deal with a producer unless he's fairly certain that exhibitors will want to show the picture. On the other hand, especially if the

picture is from an unknown production team, exhibitors may reserve the right to see the finished product before committing to playdates and number or location of theaters.

An experienced producer can attempt to retain some control over this process when he is striking his distribution agreement. In other words, he can attempt to dictate the terms of "preview" by the distributor to the exhibitor. He may create a "trailer" or "teaser" or other form of promotional clips in order to entice the exhibitor.

But (see the chapter on Exhibition) there may be legal dictates from state to state as to the terms and conditions of a distributor's pitch to exhibitors, so most distributors will demand that their marketing efforts be solely at their own discretion.

Here we get back to earlier comments about seeking sufficient commitment (financially) from a distributor to ensure that he will expend maximum effort in attaining the best possible exhibition deal.

4. **The film may be completed, distributed and exhibited, but audiences may stay away; or collection of the fair boxoffice share may be difficult to make**. You are counting on the excellence of the picture, the excellence of the marketing campaign, the positive critical acclaim, good word-of-mouth amongst audiences, and the clout of the distributor in collecting monies owed to you. In fairness to any private investor, you must disclose the hard fact that even when a picture appears to be a success, there is no guarantee that profits will occur, and that if they do, they will find their way back to the investors' pocket.

The best protection for all concerned is to make an excellent picture desired by some specific movie-going public, and to create an environment around the project where *everyone* is pushing for its success.

If all these risks are disclosed to the private investor and understood, one can then proceed to outline the possible structures film funding can take.

A. *Limited Partnerships*

Probably the most popular financial structure for individuals investing in film productions is the *Limited Partnership*.

Limited Partnerships are subject to state regulations as well as certain basic federal codes, so you must be sure to check with your local regulatory agencies as well as the Securities and Exchange Commission. A qualified business attorney is probably your safest ally for research and recommendations. Many big cities also have legal publishing houses which are extremely cooperative in mailing out reprints of the relevant code points that would govern your investment instrument.

Essentially, your investors pledge a certain amount of money toward your production, and no matter what happens, they are not liable for anything beyond that. So though they are truly partners to the enterprise, the extent of their participation and liability is "limited" to the contribution of an agreed-upon amount of funds.

You, the entrepreneurial producer, are known usually as the General Partner. It is your job to operate the business affairs of the Partnership, and you are responsible for the timely and economically efficient creation of the product for which the group was created.

In the case of lawsuit or other contest, you, the "GP," are fully liable. For this reason, many producers, who prefer not to have their own personal assets on the line, elect to create a corporation—which then becomes the General Partner.

You can be an officer of the corporation, but as long as it's a legitimate corporate entity (not considered a worthless "shell" by the government), your personal assets most likely will be protected from attachment in the case of problems. Commonly, then, you are the GP and the private investors are the LPs of the overall operation known as the Limited Partnership.

When the film is completed and, hopefully, sold, the investors will continue to benefit from any income stream coming to the group, per the defining concepts of the LP that you've created.

Sometimes the assets of the LP can be sold off, the proceeds shared, and the group dissolved. Sometimes, if it was successful, the same group can come together again in a new Limited Partnership for a new production, though the prior terms and relationship need not be exactly duplicated.

A typical sharing arrangement would be: LPs put up the production money; GP takes a small amount of the funds raised (1-5%) to operate the Partnership; the film is made; the film is sold; 95-100% of the proceeds to the Partnership will go to the LPs until their initial investment is paid back; and any additional proceeds will be shared in some prior agreed-upon basis by the GP and the LPs (50-50 split after recoupment is a common formula).

The state and federal governmental regulatory codes vary according to the total amount you're raising, the number of people whom you solicit, the economic status and qualifications of the people whom you solicit, and whether you intend to solicit beyond the state in which the Partnership will be formed.

With the many changes in Tax Codes over the past 15 years, the tax benefits of Limited Partnerships have mostly disappeared. In some cases, the government might even adjudicate that your venture is not really a Partnership at all, and in that case your investors' return may be treated as regular income.

All of this must be determined by an investor's own tax advisors, and you must disclose to them this possibility in advance.

Limited Partnerships can be created with "boiler-plate" documents (standardized forms) with just the blanks filled in. Most responsible producers, however, customize each Partnership to speak directly to the project at hand. The cost of setting up a Limited Partnership, with state filings and attorney time, can range from a few thousand to more than fifty thousand dollars, depending upon the complexity of the deal and its scope.

The governmental codes become more complex with more restrictions as you seek larger and larger sums of investment money. Furthermore, only owners of the project or registered brokers may legitimately solicit funds for the Partnership.

Over the past few years, a number of small independent production companies have sprung up and actually advertised in local papers for investors. Other groups have put a staff of people on the phones and set up a "boiler room"-type operation for cold calling to purchased or borrowed mailing lists. Though there are some circumstances where this is allowed, most such operations have either gone bankrupt or been shut down for actual or possible fraud.

While there are thousands of instances of people never receiving their money back (not to mention the film never being completed), there are some Partnerships that have found a niche, succeeded at least once, maintained a sense of responsibility regarding care for the rights of the investor as well as the quality of the film, and thus have the undying loyalty of their investors.

The "pride of ownership" factor can be high for film production Limited Partnerships, and if you chose to go this route, I would recommend that you spend the monies you've raised in an even more responsible fashion than you'd spend your own funds. You will be doing a service not only to your investors, but to the entire field of independent film production financing.

B. Corporate Entities

Though a corporation usually cannot invest as a "Limited Partner," it sometimes wishes to participate in the financing of a feature film. There might be a product or service or issue presented in the picture that the corporation considers would benefit it. There could be employment or promotional advantages to the home community or some other public relations value from a particular film investment.

However, the corporation does not want to have its assets at stake, so such an investment must be carefully structured with all proper insurance and other protections in place. A large corporation may have a "Public Relations" or "Community Relations" division, or even a "Foundation," that feels a responsibility to back a picture. (A notable recent example is ARCO's support of *Stand and Deliver.*)

If you believe that your project would directly benefit a corporation, you should first identify who the potential corporate investor is, then show how your film's message aligns with the general promotional or service thrust of the corporation.

Your presentation to the corporation usually includes the script, budget, assurances of distribution and exhibition likelihood, and even a detailed description of a publicity campaign that would promote the group's involvement with the project. The corporation may be willing to put up not only cash, but products or "in-kind" services as well.

There are "product placement" firms that seek and find companies that wish to have their product along with a screen credit displayed in your movie, in exchange for a payment of monies or other support.

C. Private Placements

If the investment package you create for your film project is considered worthy of formal presentation by a licensed broker or "registered representative" (who works either independently or for a stock brokerage firm) to a known and highly qualified investment public, you may elect for the broker to make personal calls to a limited group of individuals in his efforts to secure financing for your film.

Each state in the U.S. has rules and guidelines governing what constitutes a "qualified investor" and how many presentations can be made. The less administrative and legal red tape you wish to go through, the more stringent are the qualifications that your potential investor public must meet. Your broker should be familiar with these requirements in any state where he intends to make these "private placements."

Should an investor wish to participate in financing your project, he will have to sign an affidavit concerning his income and net worth, so most brokers prefer to approach select trustworthy prospects with whom they have done business previously.

High-income individuals will often group together and pool their resources for investments that are not widely available to the general public. They may hire an investment advisor to seek projects in which they can participate and can gain substantial ownership. Such groups make ideal targets for "private placement" film ventures.

The trick, of course, is finding them and learning what their own funding criteria are and then determining how your project could best be presented. There are various listings in financial guidebooks, magazines, professional business journals and even the phone book for investment advisors and entrepreneurial groups to approach with your package. Most of them expect a fully professional presentation with a legally valid document.

One difficulty with these types of solicitations is that each side must confirm the legitimacy of the other, and that can take considerable investigation. An even greater difficulty is that most experienced investor groups like this expect to examine not only the quality of your project, but a "projection" of your expected results.

A projection is a forecast of anticipated revenues from your film. This is usually stated in the form of a "Business Plan" or "Executive Summary." (Models of such documents are available in business books at libraries and bookstores.)

However, as emphasized elsewhere in this book, it is risky to predict a film's revenue. The only valid prediction would be based on pre-selling the film for cash, and that leads to the other problems mentioned above about "fragmentation" of rights.

Furthermore, there are federal codes regarding "projection" of returns in any investment solicitation package. In effect, these codes state that if one is going to mention the upside, one must equally mention the downside; if one is going to quote the good boxoffice performance of any past similar movies, then one must quote examples of "flops" as well.

While seemingly restrictive on the one hand, the purpose of these codes is to protect gullible investors from putting their money into a glamorous project without fully understanding the risks. Also, it's the purpose of these codes to protect you from future claims of misrepresentation or fraud by your financial partners.

Even though it may seem to put a damper on your project, it is certainly a good idea to follow the rules and regulations of the industry early in the game. If your production is a good bet, it should stand the test of legal scrutiny and still seem appealing. One experienced Hollywood producer has said, "I've never been involved in a production that didn't have one or more lawsuits associated with it." Perhaps you can avoid that expensive and humiliating quagmire.

D. Registered Public Offerings

When you are seeking either lots of money, or money from many prospective investors, it may be necessary to register your offering with a state and/or federal regulatory body (local State Commissioner of Corporations, Securities and Exchange Commission, etc.). If you wish to have a licensed stockbroker or investment advisor sell shares of your investment, you may have to register any promotional materials with the National Association of Securities Dealers or some other brokerage regulator.

While brokers may, in some cases, be willing to sell an unregistered investment product as a private placement, their own "due diligence" departments (the division of their firm that investigates the soundness of any investment product they sell) may require a formal inspection.

Furthermore, any advertisement or promotional literature you issue will fall under possible scrutiny by these bodies, all of which maintain strict guidelines concerning what you can and cannot say in your solicitation or advertising materials.

The registered public offering is a more suitable form of investment structure for high-budget feature films, or packages of several films, or as a distribution and P&A fund for several projects. However, over the past few years, several low-budget independent producers have attempted public offerings for $1 million pictures.

A danger is that legal and administrative costs along with brokerage commissions can eat up 8–20% of the funds you've collected.

One way around some of this can be to utilize the service of "finders." A finder is an individual who can identify or "find" prospective investors for you and connect you up directly with the prospect. A finder, unless he is a registered representative or an owner of the project, cannot discuss the business aspect of your film, and certainly cannot talk about the potential profitability of it lest he, too, become liable for the future complaints of any disgruntled investors.

So if you have lots of well-meaning friends who are trying to steer money to your film, do inform them that they will be serving as finders only, and that they are not to paint a glorious picture of all the profits in store for the investor. In exchange for standard "finding," you can offer a percentage of the money they have found and you have closed.

However, you must also disclose to the investor that part of his funds will not be going "on the screen," but will be paid out to finders and other brokers. This is usually done by enclosing a "budget top sheet" (summary of the major categories of expense associated with your movie) with your investment prospectus.

The key point in all of this is the idea of "disclosure." Consider that the government feels it must take the side of the uninformed investor. It plays the role of the watchdog in regulating any public request for funds.

If you disclose all possible risks, including conflict of interest (for example, if you're taking a salary from the funds raised, then you're benefiting whether or not your investor ever gets back a cent), then you're being a responsible solicitor of funds. If you're painting too pretty a picture or not disclosing all possible risks and conflicts of interest, then you will inevitably be called upon to answer for misrepresentation, misleading advertising, and worst of all, outright fraud.

Believe it or not, there are still interested investors in movies even after you disclose the risks—people who can afford the loss, or believe enough in the project their sense of "pride of owner-ship" prevails. And they might even make some money!

EXHIBITORS

In the past, if a movie was "hot" enough (big stars, big director, lots of innovative special effects, very topical subject, very popular genre), exhibitors (theater-owners) might ante up cash to guaran-tee their rights to show the film. This was still risky for the exhibitor, who might not make a profit or even meet the added cost of this advance to his weekly expenses.

So an exhibitor would only do this if he had strong reason to believe the film would be highly desirable. This was most often the case when elements of proven box-office appeal were included in the picture, such as sequels to successful movies.

Also, in order to avoid "blind bidding" restraints (see sections on "Distribution" and "Exhibition"), in some states, the exhibitor might have recourse to recoup some of his advance to the producer if the film performed poorly.

In the 1970's, some over-zealous exhibitors, in a race to lock-in the rights to show an anticipated hit film, came up with so much cash in advance to the producers and distributors that they went bankrupt. Since then, the governmental lobby for exhibitors has been pushing for restraints on these kinds of practices.

Nonetheless, a fledgling producer of an innovative or desirable film can go directly to the exhibitor—especially an independent local one—bypassing distributors, and cutting a better deal than through standard distribution channels. Whether this includes cash in advance, or some higher-than-average profit-sharing split, would depend on the producer's negotiating powers.

Again, all these modes of production financing call for qualified legal advice to protect the interests of everyone concerned.

CHAPTER 3

BUDGETING AND FINANCING

While obviously the more a picture costs to make the more it will have to produce in revenues to pay back the investors, there are many subtleties relating the overall cost of production to the "break-even" performance level. Primary amongst these is the "above-the-line" and "below-the-line" ratios.

ABOVE-THE-LINE AND BELOW-THE-LINE

Above-the-line refers to the "talent" costs of a movie—typically the producer, director, writer and actors. *Below-the-line* refers to the "goods and services" costs of a movie—typically all the hardware (cameras, lights, sound gear, editing gear, costumes, sets, props, etc.), software (supplies for the hardware, such as film, makeup, and all the expendable accessories), and craftspeople associated with a film.

Note that experienced above-the-line people are usually protected by the covenants of the talent guilds (Directors Guild of

"A TOUCH OF ETERNITY"
(Final Working Budget)

ACCT#	DESCRIPTION	PAGE #			TOTAL
101	Story & Other Rights	1			0
102	Producer	1			0
103	Director's Unit	1			0
104	Cast	1			0
105	Bits	1			0
106	Extras	2			0
107	FRINGES				0
	TOTAL ABOVE-THE-LINE	2			0
201	Production Staff	2			0
202	Set Construction	3			0
203	Set Operations	3			0
204	Special Rigging	4			0
205	Set Dressing	4			0
206	Property	4			0
207	Wardrobe	4			0
301	Makeup & Hairdressing	5			0
302	Electrical Department	5			0
303	Camera Operations	6			0
304	Sound Operations	6			0
305	Transportation	6			0
306	Location	7			0
307	Prod. Film & Laboratory	7			0
401	FRINGES				0
	TOTAL PRODUCTION PERIOD	8			0
402	Editing	8			0
403	Music	9			0
404	Post Production Sound	9			0
405	Post Production Film & Lab.	9			0
406	Main & End Titles	10			0
501	FRINGES	10			0
	TOTAL EDITING PERIOD	10			0
601	Insurance	10			0
602	Miscellaneous	11			0
701	FRINGES	11			0
	TOTAL OTHER CHARGES	11			0
	TOTAL BELOW-THE-LINE				0
	TOTAL ABOVE & BELOW-THE-LINE				0
	FRINGES (included in above)				0
	Contingency				0
	GRAND TOTAL				0

America, Writers Guild of America, Screen Actors Guild), and below-the-line people are usually protected by the rules and regulations of the craft unions (IATSE, NABET). The various written agreements of these groups can be requested directly from them, or found summarized in *Brooks' Standard Rate Book*.)

In addition to above- and below-the-line costs, a movie's budget usually includes some operating and indirect costs of production, such as overhead for the production company, a contingency of approximately 10% to cover any unanticipated expenses, legal fees, and, in the case of privately financed movies, an allowance for finders' fees, commissions, and the like.

The sum of these three general categories of expense is known as *the bottom line*, and represents the total cost to produce the film and deliver a completed negative with image, sound and titles, ready for having copies made for distribution and exhibition. This total sum is sometimes called *the negative cost*.

Most film investors will look for a justifiable relationship between the above- and below-the-line totals. For example, on a low-budget film, the above-the-line talent should not be paid huge sums (say, 50% of the total), leaving inadequate funds for the actual goods and services required to make a professional picture.

Conversely, they should not be paid so little they will suffer during production, and have their attention on the next job needed to pay their ordinary living expenses. I have seen low-paid crew members spend every coffee and lunch break on the phone calling their agent or prospective new employers. This is demoralizing to the rest of the crew and can lead to a "who cares" attitude.

Over-enthusiastic producers can think it's smart to get a crew to work "on spec" (speculating that the picture will be sold and they'll eventually be paid), saving investors' money. But I would discourage this practice, as when the going gets rough, the hours and shooting schedules long and intense, mutiny may arise among the crew, undermining cost- and time-effective production. Also, be on guard for a wide-eyed but inexperienced crew willing to work for free or on spec. When exhaustion sets in, these commitments are rarely remembered.

Generally an acceptable ratio is about 1/3 above-the-line and 2/3 below-the-line on films budgeted up to about $3 million. Unacceptable ratios on each side of this are not uncommon— 1/10 above and 9/10 below, or 1/2 above and 1/2 below.

An experienced film investor should inspect the budget summary to ensure that there are sufficient funds allotted to both production sectors, and in balanced relation to each other. This is a specialized skill, and an investor who is unfamiliar with film budgets should hire a seasoned producer or production manager to give an opinion. If the professional opinion is widely at variance with the submitted budget top-sheet, the investor is well within his rights to query the funds-seeker and ask that he justify his budget summary.

On higher-budgeted films, it is common to see an ever greater proportion of the negative cost go to above-the-line talent. Above the $3–4 million level, higher-priced writers, stars and directors may be employed to ensure higher returns—from exhibitor to distributor to producer to investor.

A special case is the super-low-budgeted production (the $10,000–50,000 feature or made-for-home product shot on Super 8mm film, 16mm film, or even video) where the entrepreneurial producer has talked his cast and crew into "working on deferment" which in essence means throwing their cards in the pool on the bet that the film, once shot and edited, can be sold right away, at least for video release, with the participants paid out of first proceeds, even before the investors have recouped.

There are cases of success with this style of filmmaking, but usually only when it's a genre picture with a very short shooting schedule (7–10 days).

In years past, vendors such as labs and equipment rental houses would occasionally become unwitting co-investors by lending their goods and services to such a production. Unfortunately, very few of these projects ever paid off, and most vendors will no longer participate on a deferment basis, unless they feel or can be convinced they are gaining some other highly valuable exchange.

There is sufficient film and video production activity today, at least in Hollywood, that the old argument—"your equipment is sitting on the shelf anyway"—is no longer a valuable inducement for this kind of sponsorship.

Since theatrical exhibition can rarely be guaranteed for any film project, you might try to peg the production budget at a level where you feel that for a film of its particular category, with whatever name or production value it has going for it, it can recoup its costs from all the other markets available to it outside of theatrical.

OPPORTUNITIES FOR PARTIAL FINANCING

Another relevancy of above- and below-the-line figures has to do with investment groups that will back one side, pending your ability to secure the other. For example, if a group owns a production facility which currently needs utilization, they may offer to back your below-the-line if you can secure above-the line.

In effect, they may not be putting up cash, but rather merely the utilization of stages, equipment and personnel which they already have under employ. Also, with their buying power, they may be able to cut far better deals from local vendors for goods and services than you can alone as an independent.

This is a tricky area in that your investors for above-the-line ought to know exactly what the below-the-line funders have put up, since this will become relevant if and when any revenues are realized. Usually, both sides feel they have put up the make/break portion of your funding and will vie to be in a first position to collect their share from any revenues. The adage of "first in-first out" does not hold up when the second batch of funds or support put into your project considers that it has made it "a go."

When you accede to partial financing, you are opening up a huge area of negotiations, since the source of any remaining funds will justifiably think that they ought to be given due consideration since their "finishing" monies have really enabled you to start to commence production, or, at least, to complete it. The first funders in your project will justifiably consider that they showed their faith initially when there was no guarantee of anything, and they, thus, ought to be rewarded with first funds out.

In addition to this complexity, it can also be the case that neither side really puts up cash, but rather puts up a promise, pending your meeting other conditions. In fact, it may be that the promising group or individual really has no assets, but will then use the second funding group's promise to secure their own financial manipulations.

Sometimes the first group will assert that they will put up X dollars in exchange for certain specified rights to your film, such as U.S. video. Since the rights they'll want are usually the most valuable ones, this fragmentation may cripple your later negotiations for distribution.

So do not hastily accept partial funding for your picture if (a) no real cash is put up, or (b) the desired rights in exchange for partial funding are so attractive that you retain no bargaining power to get your second batch of funds.

Above all, it would be prudent to check out fully any individual or group who attempts to offer you partial funding. Just as they will want to know your skills and the strength of the project, you have every right to know their real ability to deliver the promised monies for a fair exchange. You need to be convinced that your own entrepreneurial drive is not being exploited for someone else's unfair gain.

CHAPTER 4

KEEPING THE PRODUCTION ON TRACK

T he purpose of accounting, or keeping records of the inflow and outflow of funds on your project, should be to provide an orderly running record of all expenses associated with a film. Unfortunately, it all too often becomes "creative accounting," and sometimes is used to short-change the producer or investors.

The sections below, describing the production responsibilities of various posts on a film crew, are not intended to provide exhaustive definitions but rather to discuss how these functions relate to the overall financial well-being of a movie project.

PRODUCTION POSTS

The Producer. In the "golden age" of Hollywood, when the major studios reigned supreme, the "producer of record" of a film was the studio itself. It most often would assign a "house producer" to the project.

A typical house producer would be in charge of several films at a time, reporting to the assigned studio executive. An "associate producer," whose main function was to coordinate postproduction activities, reported to the producer. Since most of the above- and below-the-line individuals were being paid a salary, not too much attention was put on the daily costs of the show, as long they were within the budget.

It was assumed that the producer, production manager and production accountant were "doing their thing," which was aimed at satisfying the studio bosses.

In today's independent, entrepreneurial climate, each project is more of an "event," with the key administrative posts becoming their own little seats of power, looking out for their own good. Today's producer will often take a large fee rather than a salary, accompanied by perquisites, or "percs." Percs include extra benefits, such as insurance, office staff, expense account, performance incentives (greater rewards the more money the picture makes), and the like.

The Production Manager. The production manager or "p.m." is the key liaison between administrative and creative affairs on a film project. He is charged with the responsibility of hiring and firing vendors and many of the below-the-line crew, creating the budget, and breaking down the script into a realistic and cost-effective shooting schedule.

Sometimes the production manager may tend to play the two sides against one another, positioning himself as the deal-maker and referee in all possible conflicts, whereas he himself may actually be the source of many of them!

On one movie, the p.m. was in collusion with the producer to cheat the director out of a performance incentive. The director had negotiated a deal giving him a big bonus if the picture came in on-time and under-budget.

When it looked as if he was going to meet those targets, the p.m. arranged for a fancy catered lunch one day toward the end of shooting—which cost just enough to drive the picture over-budget! The director didn't get his bonus and later found out that the p.m. had gotten a percentage from the producer of what the director's bonus would have been had he come in under-budget.

Although this type of blatant criminality doesn't pervade the industry, it is always a possibility when such large amounts of dollars are at stake.

On another picture, the p.m. cut a deal where he would get a percentage of any savings he could garner from the line items on the approved budget. So if there were, say, $15 per day per person for meals, he would tell a local vendor he had $10 per day to spend, and if they could beat that he'd ensure they could be extras in the film, or get their name in the credits.

In many cases, the vendors went for this, and the p.m. got a share of the difference. It was the crew who lost out, having to eat inferior meals. Eventually the crew became so upset they rebelled and demanded steak dinners at restaurants. This was paid for out of a contingency fund, and the p.m. still got to keep his percentage of the "line item" savings.

With games like this running rampant in parts of the film industry, you can see that both crew and investors lose out, since such shooting circumstances end up affecting the quality of the film. So the investors need an ally—ideally, the producer.

The Production Accountant. The production accountant, whose neutrality ought to be sacred, should be a friend to the investor. The investor may even want to reserve the right to select the production accountant. Ideally, the reason an investor comes into a project in the first place is because of trust and confidence in the producer. It follows that the crew the producer selected would be equally trustworthy.

On most productions, the accountant turns in a daily and weekly "cost report." Both producer and investor should be apprised of the budget status frequently. The producer should be responsible for both the best possible film and the most prudent expenditures of available production funds.

The p.m. is his field sergeant, and should ensure that crew morale is high and productivity, from a time standpoint, is optimum. The accountant should not only keep excellent records, but be able to spot imbalances, potential cost overruns, and brewing legal or code situations (union agreements, location licenses and fees, set security, thievery, breakage, etc.).

The Associate Producer. If the post of associate producer used to be that of a postproduction coordinator, today it is mainly as an honorary position, a carrot on a stick for either the writer or a friend of the producer or director. (It is one of the few ways a writer can justifiably be invited to the set.)

This is not necessarily bad, in that the associate producer can become an "observer," the eyes and ears of the producer or director, from a creative standpoint. Since the producer is often involved with the director and actors or money people, and since the director always is on the set shooting, there is a real need for a departmental coordinator, somebody who can troubleshoot potential creative problems.

In a traditional business activity which results in a product for consumption, there is always, or should always be, a "quality control" position. Film productions rarely have such a person, relying on a sort of shared responsibility.

While this may be the case with a highly experienced production team that has worked together often, it would be a boon to most modern independent productions to have a quality control, or department coordination, position, occupied by someone entirely trusted by the producer and/or director. This person should not be burdened with business details or administrative affairs, as the p.m. often is.

So the associate producer might ideally understand the creative goals of the project, and have sufficiently good rapport with the producer and/or director to file daily, sometimes hourly, reports on the status of the creative departments.

Ultimately, the primary budget consideration is that every possible production dollar ends up on the screen. This includes not only excellent image and sound due to equipment, props and other physical qualities of the production, but high crew morale through fair pay and considerate working conditions.

The combination of the right tools for the job and a high-performance cast and crew *is* achievable, but doesn't happen by accident or luck. It happens through proper planning and full responsibility being shared by everyone. A winning production means success and that means more work for each member of the production unit.

Any signs of disgruntlement or unethical behavior should be spotted and eliminated before preproduction begins. But if any rears up once shooting commences, it must be handled thoroughly. Your willingness to demand up-front group excellence as a condition of signing up with the crew may mean that you never have to raise your voice during production. Then the investor can expect that his money is being well-tended.

INSURANCE

In addition to competent crews, organized productions and a completion bond, the investor's final protection comes in the form of an insurance policy.

In many municipalities in the U.S., you *must* legally have insurance to be allowed to film. Many low-budget independent projects have attempted to bootleg their work, or side-step the approved methods of attaining permissions. While it may appear to be a cost-saving step, since insurance can cost as much as 6% of the film's overall budget, it is not a wise move in today's litigation-crazed production climate.

Besides, any time you knowingly break the law, it comes back to haunt you. It is certainly not acceptable to film on an investor's funds without doing everything you can to safeguard the project.

There is only a handful of companies that underwrite film insurance policies, and of those, only a few will take on low-budget projects; the premiums are often just not enough to cover the cost of the insurance broker's or agent's paperwork.

However, there are some excellent companies in the major cities that do specialize in working with independents, especially if the production team has any kind of proven track record. (My own production company has been with the same insurance group for more than 10 years. During this time, they've honored a number of claims without any unjustified increase in rates.)

There are many kinds of film production insurance, every one with its own premium rate basis. Each must be evaluated against the circumstances of your project to determine which you need. Your insurance agent is usually an excellent source of information and can make recommendations based on industry standards. You may also wish to check with experienced producers to see which type of insurance has been most useful on his projects.

Taken from a typical film production insurance policy, here is a brief listing and description of the major categories of coverage:

Negative Insurance. Negative insurance reimburses the production company for any loss or damage to developed or undeveloped negative film, sound tracks or original videotape elements.

Faulty Stock, Camera or Processing. This form of insurance reimburses the production company for any losses resulting from faulty raw stock from the manufacturer, dysfunction of camera, sound or video equipment, or lab error during developing or other processing.

Props, Sets and Wardrobe. This covers you in case of destruction of, damage to, or theft of props, sets and wardrobe.

Miscellaneous Equipment. This provides coverage for loss of or damage to any camera, sound, lighting or editing equipment. In some policies, this can be extended to cover production vehicles, such as equipment trucks and vans, "honeywagons" (portable toilets), makeup and costume trucks, etc.

Cast Insurance. Should an actor or director suffer death, accident or illness during the production, this form of insurance covers losses to the company for postponement, interruption or cancellation of the shoot. The personnel covered will be required to have a physical examination, and there are doctors in most cities who specialize in these insurance check-outs.

Such coverage, if granted, will usually commence during preproduction. (There are somewhat esoteric additions to Cast Insurance, covering such things as kidnapping and ransom demands!)

Extra Expense. Reimburses the production company for additional costs related to interrupted, postponed or canceled shooting due to damage or destruction to props, sets, wardrobe, equipment or other property and facilities.

Third Party Property Damage. This vital type of coverage compensates for damage to or destruction of the property of others, such as private homes, building interiors, and other places used as film locations under the care, custody and control of the production company.

Animal Mortality Insurance. Reimburses the owner of an animal scheduled for use in production should the animal die.

Adverse Weather Insurance. In the event of high winds, excessive cloud cover or precipitation, this type of insurance reimburses the production company in case of a canceled day of filming. Adverse weather coverage must be planned for specific days and locations substantially in advance of the scheduled shoot.

Workers' Compensation. Whether or not you hire union crews or independent contractors, you are required by most states to carry Workers' Compensation. Anyone working on your production will usually be held to be an employee, and thus is entitled to this coverage. Failure to carry it can result in the non-payment of benefits, and penalties as well.

Comprehensive Liability. Provides coverage to the production company against claims for bodily injury and property damage liability. This also covers liability arising from the use of non-owned vehicles. Any municipality in which you work will require evidence of this coverage, naming the municipality as a "loss payee" and/or as an "additional insured," prior to their issuing you a permit to film there.

Errors & Omissions. If you intend to have your work shown publicly through film distributors, television networks, syndicators or other forms of exhibition, you will be required to carry Errors & Omissions ("E&O") insurance. This provides coverage for your legal liability and defense arising from lawsuits alleging unauthorized use of titles, ideas, characters, plots; plagiarism; invasion of privacy; libel; slander; defamation of character; etc.

It is usually purchased at the same time as production insurance, although it sometimes can be acquired just prior to a distribution deal closing. Many insurance companies, however, will not sell you E&O unless you've bought your other insurance from them as well.

Generally, you can insure individual productions, or, if you're going to make a series of shorter or lower-budgeted documentaries, commercials or videos, you can buy a package policy covering your complete production work for the year. Such a package policy is subject to audit by the insurance company, and if you've exceeded your limits, you'll be charged an additional premium at year end. If you've come in under your predicted production expenses for the year, you may get a rebate.

In any case, you can see that insurance exists for all types of hazards associated with film or video production. It is a relatively low price to pay for the peace of mind you'll gain for yourself and your investors.

BOOK
TWO

DISTRIBUTION

DISTRIBUTION

Definition: *making a completed film or videotape available to the markets and venues that may wish to sell or exhibit it, in exchange for an agreed-upon portion of the revenues.*
Result: *the film or videotape is accepted for showing or selling to the widest possible target audience with the most favorable financial terms for both the distributor and the producer.*

CHAPTER 5

THE DISTRIBUTION GAME

D istribution occupies the middle position in the film industry production and selling cycle: production-**distribution**-exhibition.

As with every capitalistic business since the industrial revolution, the "middleman" has become necessary due to the sheer volume of products and consumers. Just as very few farmers can truck their carrots straight to the markets for selling any more, few filmmakers or videomakers can truck their prints and cassettes directly to theaters or video stores.

Aside from not having enough equipment and personnel, there is a seemingly endless stream of administrative tasks involved—dealmaking, contracts, inspections, collections, etc. Furthermore, there is a technology to film distribution, involving such variables as geography, season, demographics of target audience, and negotiation based on other and future holdings of the distribution company.

So most producers have not found it viable to create their own internal distribution networks.

In theory, and occasionally in fact, a film or videomaker could produce a work at a sufficiently low cost that it would be cost-effective for him to drive the print directly to a theater for its play dates, then collect the funds from the theater owner or manager on an agreed-upon split. A video could be so low-cost that taking a few crates of them to his local video stores, not to mention direct sales through the mails, could return a profit. This is the exception.

As with any business system where there is a middleperson serving as a conduit for the product to the consumer, there is the chance to intelligently control the flow, as well as the danger of manipulation on either side.

As discussed earlier, before the Paramount Consent Decree, the Hollywood studios essentially controlled their own distribution to their own theaters. Collections were rarely a problem since the theater managers were virtual employees of the producers. But with the splitting off of theater ownership from the major distributors, battles have raged between film investors, producers and distributors on one side and exhibitors on the other.

Since the distributor is the producer's first level of connection to his paying audience, today's professional filmmaker must learn about this often misunderstood and maligned functionary.

THE MAJORS

Those distribution networks still owned and controlled by the large motion picture studios are known as "the majors." They maintain offices and staff nationwide and, sometimes, internationally. They distribute films made not only by their affiliated studios, but they purchase or "pick up" films made by independent producers as well. Whereas a major studio may produce only 10–15 films per year, the major distributors may handle 30 or more.

The overhead cost of operating and maintaining a nationwide or worldwide distribution network is huge. Between payroll, rent, insurance, and immense phone, FAX and other communications costs, the major distributors can have monthly "nuts," or operating costs, of millions of dollars.

Add to this the cost of film prints, videocassettes, advertising (even if shared on a cooperative basis with producer or exhibitor) and other promotions (junkets to film festivals and film markets), and you can see that a major distributor must ensure it receives a healthy fee and/or percentage of the proceeds from each picture it handles.

As in the other economics-driven arts, the filmmaker is often confronted with the choice of either going with a big distribution company for prestige, even if he gets a smaller piece of the pie, or choosing a boutique distributor who will give more personalized service, but may not have the clout with exhibitors.

Having made a film considered worthy of major distribution regardless of immediate financial gains can be worth its weight in gold when you get ready to make your next one. Now you have a track record. You're in the "club" of feature filmmakers who have a proven sense of audience that aligns with the majors' market

69

sensibility. This fact alone could make you "bankable" for subsequent projects.

The trade-off, of course, is that the distribution expenses of the major are so high that you may never see profits, and this is a big disappointment to you and your investors.

For this reason, many entrepreneurial producers tell their private investors that by financing their first picture, they'll be in a "first position" to be involved in any subsequent productions. The unstated "carrot on a stick" is: "Don't worry, if you get screwed on this one, but it's successful nonetheless, you'll get it all back and more on our next deal when *we're* in the driver's seat. Because we're now known as suppliers of high-grade product."

Another liability of working through major distributors is the difficulty of auditing their financial records. Considering the large number of projects they handle each year, it is not uncommon for a major distributor to apply profits from one picture against losses from another. This "cross-collateralization" is responsible for much of the distrust and unrest amongst producers, and it becomes a negotiating point when establishing a distribution deal.

Cross-collateralization is but one of the numerous complexities in determining whether you want to align with a distributor. As mentioned earlier, one major distributor's contractual definition of "net profit" is 12 legal size single-spaced typed pages!

For reasons like this, many producers hold off as long as possible before establishing a distribution arrangement. They test the waters and determine what the range of going prices will be for their film. The further along they are into production, the more favorable the distribution arrangement will usually be, because the distributor can see more of a finished product and is taking less of a chance in committing to the picture.

It has been stated that there are two ideal relationships to a distributor, from the viewpoint of a producer.

The first would be this: Distributor pays the producer enough of an advance to ensure the distributor will work hard to get its money back; then accounts honestly each quarter or six months as to revenues and exact itemized expenses, with the first six months paying back the advance, and the next 12 to 18 months paying out enough to cover continuing distribution expenses and fees with additional monies being profits to the producer.

This would be the second one: Producer essentially hires distributor for a set weekly or monthly fee, thereby reducing distributor's risk to virtually nothing, but perhaps running a slight danger of not quite engaging the distributor's full interest since there's nothing particularly at stake as he's not a profit participant. To offset this latter risk, a producer may try to get the distributor to agree to some sort of performance guarantee.

This producer-distributor relationship is one of the trickiest in the entire film industry. In fact, some distributors have said in print that they assume they will be sued by disgruntled producers, so they might as well withhold funds and have that much more use and interest out of the film-generated revenues. Also, many producers will negotiate the highest possible cash advance from the distributor in exchange for a lesser percentage of profits, assuming that is all the revenues he'll ever see, short of litigation and out-of-court settlements.

MINI-MAJORS AND INDEPENDENTS

While the vast size and communication links of the major distributors is appealing to many producers, others have decided that a smaller distributor, with perhaps a specialty in a particular genre of film or area of the country or world, is more suitable to their projects.

Often, the "mini-major" or independent distributor hooks up with the majors anyway for specified market areas or media, but this doesn't directly affect the producer.

So many mini-majors went bankrupt in the 80's due to mismanagement and unreasonably large cash advances to the wrong films, that it's difficult to predict if they will remain a viable alternative for the independent producer. But since they do handle far less product each year than the majors, it's easier to pinpoint or target a smaller distributor that has specialized in the past in your type of film.

Your best method of research is to find out who distributed films similar to your own and contact them to see about their interest in another such project. You might also contact the credited producers of such films to see if they feel they got a fair accounting and proceeds from the distributor.

One technique used by the smaller independents is the hiring of specialists in certain geographic areas of the country—*regional subdistributors*—who are familiar with the filmgoing patterns in that sector. The fees or percentages paid out to these subdistributors is often more than recompensed by their expertise at understanding the needs of specific audiences, and by their familiarity with local exhibitors.

There is no reason why a producer who has not yet made an overall distribution deal for his picture shouldn't contact a regional subdistributor on his own, and make a short-term deal for one area of the country where he anticipates success for his project. A way to contact such a group, other than the usual production guidebooks, would be to contact theaters in the targeted area who have shown films similar to yours and ask where they received the films.

You could also ask which local distributors seem to be most cooperative and supportive in terms of advertising and coordinating other promotional efforts.

If you're successful in setting up a regional deal, you either may find it so profitable that you decide to approach the whole country that way and not worry about big splashy New York or Los Angeles openings; or you'll gain a good enough track record in one area, including not only boxoffice but critical response and positive audience word of mouth, that you can then approach a major distributor and attempt to sell off the rest of the country and world at more favorable terms than you would have received before this demonstration of your film's drawing power.

THE TECHNOLOGY OF FILM DISTRIBUTION

While film distribution has a public reputation as a "hit or miss" enterprise, there are a surprisingly large number of accepted, persistent truths about its technology. Knowledge of these is one of the main reasons you're paying the distributor his fee.

Among these stable realities are: seasonal variables, audience demographics, and theater patronage patterns. Here is a brief description of some of the considerations in these areas.

Seasonal Variables. One of the most enduring of all facts about the film industry is seasonal movie attendance patterns.

U.S. FILM ATTENDANCE

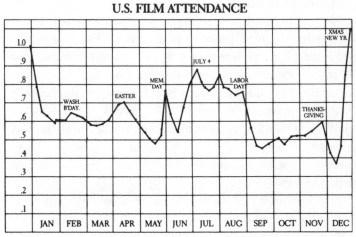

This pattern repeats year after year, decade after decade, with small variations. Note that the Christmas period is by far the highest two-week attendance period, and summer is easily the highest season. Also note the valleys of movie attendance after

73

Christmas through Easter, and after Labor Day when school summer vacation ends through Thanksgiving.

With full knowledge of this, the major producers and distributors will target certain kinds of films (based on genre and theme) for certain show dates. This is why you hear so often about a film being completed and then waiting six months for release.

This also means that there will be a glut of "big" adventure and fantasy films during the Summer and Christmas seasons, and fewer "serious" or adult-themed films at these times. Occasionally there is an exception, such as *Dead Poets Society*, which surprised all the analysts by being a "big and serious and adult-themed" release for Christmas, and doing great boxoffice business. After the fact, it was understood to be a marketing coup since the picture starred Robin Williams, was about kids and schools, had the Disney imprimatur, and drew the interest of the 30–45-year-old audience who had not much else by way of mature programming to attend.

Also, occasionally, a major will release an uncertain film a week before the prime seasons hoping that good word-of-mouth will make it "the" picture to go to as soon as school lets out. *Star Wars* was an excellent example of this marketing ploy.

Another fact you can deduce from these seasonal patterns is that small independent pictures will probably get lost in the shuffle if released at these prime times, not to mention their difficulty in getting into key upscale theaters. Summer and Christmas bookings in theaters often run one year in advance or more.

So a distributor that earns its fee will not only try to get your picture to the right theater, but at the right time.

Audience Demographics. Attempts have been made, usually unsuccessfully, to apply traditional marketing survey techniques from other industries to film. There have been many formulas but few seemed to have held up. Because of this, the motion picture industry is notorious for depending on audience whim, and its resolute refusal to use surveys to find out what people want to see.

One of the fabled exceptions to this rule was *First Blood*, the first "Rambo" film. European film audiences were allegedly surveyed to determine what the "essential adventure picture" ought to contain. Notably, *First Blood* was not only an enormous success in America, but world-wide.

About the only traditional use of surveys in the film business is to determine what kind of publicity campaign to go with once the picture is already completed. A distributor will often prepare two or three ad campaigns for the same picture, and test market the film in different but comparable cities to see which enticed the most viewers to attend.

A classic example of this technique was *Out of Africa*, which was released with both an adventure-themed and a love story-themed campaign. The love story approach brought in more satisfied movie-goers, so the adventure-themed campaign was eventually reduced, and in some areas of the country eliminated altogether.

The most sophisticated film marketeers currently consider there are four discreet and finite movie-going audiences: younger men, younger women, older men, older women. Apparently each tends to patronize different movie theaters during different seasons, on different nights of the week. Of course they also favor different types of films. Young men, for example, prefer adventure, sci-fi, comedies and super-heroes, whereas older men tend to prefer war movies and films depicting realistic violence.

You can see how every element of distribution—from ad campaigns and other promotions to preferred theaters and release dates—would be affected by this information.

Another intriguing concept was generated by a *Film Comment* magazine survey, in which they interviewed people coming out of the theaters showing any one of the 10 most popular films of the year. In a startlingly high number of cases, these audience members had seen only *that* film. In other words, they hadn't seen any other of the highest money-making films of the year.

If this is true, it implies that it is a misnomer to talk about "the public," or even "the film-going public." This survey suggests that there are at least 10 movie-going publics, each one potentially large enough to make a film one of the most successful of the year.

Add this data to the four age and gender groups above and you have the beginning of a science of film distribution. Properly analyzed and understood, this information should also trickle back to producers, and begin to give them some parameters as to how much money to spend on a film's production and still maintain reasonable hope of recouping their investment.

Theater Patronage and Release Patterns. It is said that Woody Allen will allow his films to open only at certain specific theaters in New York City. It is said that the producers of the James Bond series insist their films follow an exact release pattern to key theaters in the major metropolitan areas.

True or not, these tales demonstrate the importance that producers put on precise distribution methods.

Considering that 75% or more of a film's advertising budget will be spent by the first two weekends of a film's release in a geographic area (based on the assumption that word-of-mouth had better be positive by then if the film is to be a success), you can see how vital it is to attend to a carefully planned release. Your film's distributor should be conversant if possible with successful patterns of works similar to yours.

There are several traditional ways of releasing a film, and more will surely be devised as the technology is further refined. See if any of these make sense for your particular project, then find a distributor who, at reasonable terms hopefully with a cash advance, will agree and will be familiar enough with this style that it can promise you a professional and committed execution of the plan.

(I am indebted to Richard di Giovanni for the simplicity and outline of the major distributor release patterns.)

DISTRIBUTION BY SATURATION

Basic philosophy: open the film in as many theaters simultane-ously as you possibly can. In the 1980's this number ranged from 1,700 to 2,000+.

Advertising thrust: must be supported with a large quantity of national and local advertising, publicity and other promotions, all coordinated on a nationwide basis to ensure the greatest possible anticipation by the target audience.

Rationale: you'll get as many people to see the film as possible before word-of-mouth confirms or denies the expectation, and you'll get the highest possible initial cash flow.

Risk: this is the most expensive way to release a film. Nation-wide advertising can cost $5–15 million or more. Each 35mm film print will cost approximately $1,500 and each 70mm print for the big cities with appropriate projection and sound facilities can cost $10,000 or more. If word-of-mouth is poor, the saturation approach can kill you financially.

Examples: the big horror film series (*Nightmare on Elm Street, Friday the 13th*); sequels to hit pictures (*Ghostbusters*, the *Rocky* films); films with initial built-in audience interest due to prior exposure in other media (the *Superman* series, *Conan, The Barbarian* series); reissues during holiday seasons of established classics (Disney animated features, *Star Wars* reissues); films that have tested poorly but where the investment is such that the producers *must* get some money back before word-of-mouth spreads (big star extravaganzas—I'll decline naming names).

PLATFORM RELEASE

Basic philosophy: open the film in the major cities and markets (approximately 500 theaters) and continue to build on this "plat-form" by expanding in the primary markets and adding secon-dary markets as you go.

Advertising thrust: support with ads in local newspapers, radio and television, local promotions, and occasional national ads if warranted.

Rationale: if the distributor expects positive word-of-mouth based on previews and market research, the platform method is much less expensive than the saturation approach.

Risk: if word-of-mouth is poor, the whole rationale is down the drain because it will be too late to saturate the market. Platforming thus becomes a very expensive "test" of the product. Additionally, the ancillary rights to the film (videocassettes) may become less valuable.

Examples: the first *Star Wars, E.T.—The Extraterrestrial,* the first *Raiders of the Lost Ark.*

LIMITED ENGAGEMENT

Basic philosophy: open the film in just a few theaters in a few major markets (Los Angeles, New York, Chicago,) and as the critical and audience response builds, slowly add major markets and theaters.

Advertising thrust: carefully controlled local advertising and promotion, identifying exact target audiences and critics and mining them for market information.

Rationale: this form of release is customary for sophisticated American or foreign adult-themed films where the ultimate appeal, target audience and nature of the word-of-mouth are uncertain. It allows the distributor to identify the precise route for additional promotion while being thrifty in terms of advertising dollar expenditure.

Risk: the film could gain negative word-of-mouth; the target audience could fail to be properly identified; press reviews could be poor if the film is misunderstood or improperly promoted; if box-office performance is poor enough, the distributor may decide this film has such a limited appeal it is unworthy of additional exploitation.

Examples: some Woody Allen films; music concert films; "art" films such as *My Dinner with Andre, Swimming to Cambodia*; films with major stars but of uncertain target audience (*Julia, Turning Point*).

MISCELLANEOUS APPROACHES

In addition to the traditional methods mentioned above, there are unique and innovative distribution patterns which can be suited to a particular film.

Test Marketing: when a film is considered to have significant market potential, but the exact route to a major release is unknown, an independent producer will sometimes arrange for test screenings in a few minor and inexpensive markets (usually medium-sized cities or college towns) and support these with limited but highly specific local advertising.

With these results in hand, the producer can then approach a major distributor and be in a much better negotiating position. A classic example of this approach was *Porky's.* Everybody won!

Market by Market Saturation: when a film is considered to have significant appeal to specific geographic areas and demographic groups, but perhaps not to others, a producer might rely on regional sub-distributors, handpicking each one based on expertise, or might even bypass distributors altogether and deal directly with key theater owners in small and medium-sized towns and with independent theater chains in the larger cities.

This latter method is known as "four-walling" when the producer pays a rental fee directly to the theater for use of his facility in exchange for collecting all box-office revenues. One significant value of this approach is a great reduction in distribution costs in terms of film prints. One city can be worked at a time with just a handful of prints, then you go on to the next city with those same prints and, hopefully, the good results and press generated to date

79

by the film. Family pictures such as the Sunn Classics are traditionally released in this fashion.

"Classics" Marketing: for the prestigious foreign "art" film, or the occasional eccentric American movie, the "classics" approach concentrates on specific independent "art theaters"—for example, the Laemmle chain in Los Angeles. This significantly reduces advertising costs and can build an audience over time. Examples are *Das Boot, Harold and Maude,* and, initially, *Diner.*

YOUR FILM'S TOTAL VALUE

In discussing the above, we are dealing with American theatrical distribution, only one of the many exploitable values of your film. While this is certainly the richest single market your film may ultimately have, U.S. theatrical has gone from being about 75-80% of a film's final worth to being no more than 50% on average.

The explosion in value of ancillary rights to a film has spawned an entirely different way of thinking about the marketing, sale and lease or licensing of your project. In fact, whereas it used to be that without a moderately successful U.S. theatrical release, there was little hope of your film recouping its negative cost, producers now consider "worst case scenarios" with *no* U.S. theatrical release at all and compute whether or not it still may be a viable venture. In many instances it is.

Though it is difficult to assign stable values to each of these rights listed below due to rapidly changing technological realities and socio-political-economic shifts, here is a summary of the commonly exploitable markets for your film.

Domestic Theatrical. "Domestic theatrical" refers to both the U.S. and Canadian movie theater rights. This market, though diminished in the 80's as a share of total potential revenues, is still the biggest single value your film may have. It is so large that even in some other countries they refer to the U.S./Canadian market as "domestic theatrical!"

On average, domestic theatrical can account for 40-60% of your film's eventual revenues. Due to the risk involved with this market (high cost, uncertain revenues), many companies capable of domestic distribution will not take on this domain without at least some ancillary rights to cover their ad costs.

The reasoning is: any ad dollars put into a theatrical release will help any future video, cable or other markets by making the film more high-profile. In fact, there are even a number of cases in the late 80's where a film's theatrical performance was poor but it boomed in video. Evidently, potential viewers were intrigued by the ads or word-of-mouth, but not enough to attend the screenings. Instead, they decided, "We'll wait until it's out on video."

Because of this desire to back up their investment on theatrical with ancillary rights as well, domestic distributors will urge a producer to "fragment the rights" associated with their picture. This can become a watershed decision for the producer, since once the rights are fragmented, this begins a lengthy process of shopping each remaining individual right to a specialist in the area.

Foreign Theatrical. "Foreign theatrical" refers to every place in the world outside of the U.S. and Canada. Depending on your film's genre, it can account for anywhere from 15% to 40% of your total revenues. During the 70's, this market was somewhat flat in terms of growth. However, the 80's saw a tremendous increase due to a general resurgence of foreign interest in American films.

Nobody knows exactly why this is, although it probably has to do with a globalization of high-tech awareness and thus an appreciation for the sophistication of American film craft. As in the U.S., the best playtimes are during Christmas and non-school seasons.

When your film's rights become fragmented, due to the demand of a major distributor who would not otherwise be interested in your project without at least some ancillary rights included in his deal, you may end up having to shop your film internationally, country by country, market by market, medium by medium. There are film brokers who specialize in this service for independent producers, and, take a sizable percentage of the proceeds.

Most independents starting out are well-advised to deal with someone not only who is fully established in the field, but who has additional clout working on your behalf, since he represents several films at one time and can package them together for added value. The only cautionary note here is to be sure in advance, through negotiation, of what portion of a package will be yours.

Traditionally, the most lucrative countries in which to exploit American films are, in order, England, Japan, France, Italy, Germany and Australia. Hong Kong and other countries in the Orient have been especially receptive to action-adventure and/or martial arts-themed pictures.

Foreign theatrical markets, more than in America, are dominated by major exhibition chains. For this reason, it's not uncommon for your film's broker to simply get a single cash payment as a flat fee for the theatrical rights in a given country. Percentage deals are not desirable for either side, collections and auditing being a major problem due to distance and different bookkeeping customs.

Keep in mind that your film playing in a non-English speaking country must either be dubbed or subtitled. Also, local fees, duties and taxes will have to be paid, and there may be limits on how much money paid to you can leave the country where your film's theatrical rights have been sold. This is why many people who have had success in foreign distribution end up with sizable bank accounts in these countries, and end up producing pictures there.

This is especially true, and possibly desirable, in countries which give foreigners considerable tax advantages for a film

82

produced there. Some countries, and even municipalities within those countries, offer not only below-the-line services at a truly cut rate, but give as much as a three-to-one tax write-off for any advertising dollars that you spend in exploiting the film.

The rationale for this is that you are thus advertising the country's desirability as a production haven and so assisting their balance of trade, not to mention their international public relations image.

The cost of dubbing or subtitling can be high and become a negotiating point in your deal for foreign distribution. There is no set method of determining who pays for these costs, though usually a distributor will be willing to advance the monies as long as they recoup them prior to any profit or fee sharing. It is also up to the distributor to prepare foreign advertisements and negotiate with the exhibitor as to who covers those expenses.

Since the late 80's, video cassettes, cable and satellite have had a spiraling impact on the foreign rights to a film, and more and more distributors are trying to retain as many of these ancillaries as possible to enhance a film's total revenues through additional fragmentation.

One U.S. distributor has predicted to me that the satellite rights to American feature films, once "thrown in" to any distribution deal because it had negligble value, will soon become a multi-billion-dollar market.

Some foreign distributors, especially the British-based ones, have been quietly stockpiling the satellite broadcast rights to films and, due to certain peculiarities of international laws, are implicitly gaining the privilege to broadcast the film across many countries. If this is true, when you negotiate distribution rights for your picture, make sure that "satellite broadcast" is *specifically* included or excluded for an agreed-upon fee or percentage. Do not "throw it in the pot."

Access to Foreign Markets. Unless you sell or license *all* your film's rights to a major distributor, you will need access yourself or through a broker to the foreign markets.

The customary route is by attending or sending a representative to one of the "international film markets." These are, in essence, film conventions attended by producers, distributors and exhibitors from around the world. The three largest and most famous, where millions of dollars of cash can change hands in just a few days, are the American Film Market (Los Angeles, late February), Cannes (France, Spring), and MIFED (Milan, November).

There are numerous other film festivals year-round where, though more public-viewing oriented, a considerable amount of negotiating occurs. Distributors and exhibitors will often send representatives to these showcases to be on the lookout for independent films that still have available rights associated with them.

One technique used by many independent producers is to prepare a poster, pressbook, and even a video "teaser" or promotional short, and rent a booth or align with an established broker to test the waters, determine the perceived value of their project. Then they can return to their potential investors with a significantly better sense of their film's appeal.

These "markets" and festivals are glamorous and fun, and *very* hard-nosed in terms of business negotiations. It would be wise to go with a professional, lest you emerge having bargained away all kinds of undervalued rights to your film. I would also recommend that you attend one of these markets even if you do not yet have a product to sell. Your knowledge of the international film buying and selling business routine will be greatly enhanced. The American Film Market, maintaining a year-round office in Los Angeles, sells one-day and entire market passes to spectators. They are relatively expensive, but a true education, and well worth the time and expense.

Videocassettes. The 1980's saw videocassettes go from 3-4% of the overall potential market share of a film at the beginning of the decade to as much as 50% at the end. There is probably no other single technological advance to date than the VCR that has had as wide an impact on film production, distribution, exhibition and viewing patterns.

No longer does a film have to succeed at the theater boxoffice, or in fact even be theatrically released, in order to recoup its cost and make a profit. The value of a movie in the videocassette market can outweigh in profitability and certainly staying power, its value in any other single market.

Because of this, distributors usually want to maintain video-cassette rights to a film, at home or abroad or both, as an inducement to them to take the high-cost risk of a theatrical release. In fact at least in America, some distributors primarily want the video rights, and will simply sell off the theatrical rights to a specialist.

As VCRs spread through Western Europe, the Orient, and now Eastern Europe, the foreign video rights will also become highly valuable.

One of the appealing aspects to videocassette sales is that the distributor can create his own purchase, collections and returns policies. Because a finite number of tapes will be duplicated, shipped and received by a video store, the proceeds are much easier to track than film admissions.

Collections. In terms of collections, a video distributor can flex some of the same muscles that a film distributor can: "If you want the next *Star Wars* (or some similarly successful film series), you'd better pay up for the last *Rocky*." Or, "If you want the next *Star Wars* you'll also have to take 3,000 copies of this psychological masterpiece by my nephew." (See the next section of this chapter for a discussion of this practice as related to film, known as "block booking.")

Returns. A "returns" policy is whatever rule a distributor establishes as to what a video retail store or wholesaler can do with unsold or under-rented tapes. As in book publishing, the distributor needs to make *some* provision for what to do if a tape comes up far short of sales expectations.

The distributor doesn't want the store to go bankrupt or have its shelves full of low-circulation tapes. This hurts the opportunities for the distributor's upcoming films as well—no shelf space available and insufficient cash flow from rentals to allow for payment of prior invoices.

Common returns policies include: (a) store may return without charge some percentage of unsold tapes; (b) store may return any number of unsold tapes, but for credit toward future purchases only; (c) store may have 100% returns for cash.

The "100% returns" routine is what some unscrupulous video distributors utilize so that they can report "number of tapes shipped" as their sales statistics to the press. If they neglect to include the allowance for 100% returns, they are creating an inflated sense of their marketing expertise. This is allegedly what happened to some of the founders of the home video industry, but their justification was that the initial large numbers is what put home video on the map!

As a video store's shelf space is its most valuable commodity, the store owner will be sensitive to the distributor's returns guidelines, because that establishes how "current" the retailer can remain with his titles in stock.

A current controversy in the video industry is whether a store should stock more copies of fewer "smash hit" titles, or fewer copies of a wider range of offerings. The small stores are leaning in the former direction, but this also means that after the first few months of renting of hot titles, they'll need to either sell off the used tapes cheaply to make room for new releases, or return to the distributor or manufacturer a certain number of cassettes in order to create shelf space.

So a number of the major video distributors are developing policies and agreements with their key customers to allow just that.

It remains to be seen whether the distributors will junk the old tapes, create special wholesale packages for direct sale to consumers, or attempt to salvage the plastic shells or even the tape itself for re-recording purposes.

First Sale Doctrine. A key point for the film producer to keep in mind is that normally his revenues from the video market come only from the number of cassettes sold, less returns. In other words, he does not benefit at all from the popularity of the tape as a rental item.

There is a doctrine of business practice which states that whoever buys an item may do as he pleases with it, as long as he does not violate copyrights. What this means in the video world is that if I buy a cassette from you, I can rent it, lease it, resell it, or anything else I want, as long as I don't violate your copyright through unauthorized duplication.

So the key figure in which you'll be interested is how many videocassettes of your film were sold by the distributor to wholesalers or retail outlets—not how many rentals by customers occurred.

Genre Videos. Over the past decade, there have been some business cycles, especially during periods of relatively few major film releases to video, where stores will want to stock titles other than "big pictures."

Ask any video store owner, and he'll tell you that every Friday or Saturday night, after his regular customers have already seen *Batman* or the other hit films to their satisfaction, they'll ask the store owner, "Got any new horror flics (or comedies or karate films or other such popular genre)?" Because of this market need, many producers have specialized in low-budget "made-for-video" features.

In these cases, they usually do not even intend for there to be a theatrical release. The film will be shot on 16mm film, sometimes even 8mm, and transferred right to video.

The producer or distributor may also supply the stores with attention-grabbing cardboard kiosks or other displays to grab the casual renter's attention. Such films often can be made for

87

$50,000–$150,000, and there's even a book written on how to make a sellable film for $10,000!

There are two dubious aspects to this kind of film. First, there are many major film releases to video from the big studios, and the store owner may not want to give up too much space for these low-budget specials. Secondly, since there's been no theatrical release with backup advertising and promotion, any one particular low-budget quickie may never develop a following.

So unless you are perceived as a regular supplier of decent quality low-budget films who will back up your productions with some kind of promotion or store displays and favors, the store owner may elect not to take the chance and waste the space.

Therefore, being the producer of a "one-shot-quickie" may not be as wise as it has sometimes seemed to the independent and entrepreneurial filmmaker. A $10,000 film without a market or sales outlet is a lost $10,000 for someone.

Free Television. Free television, usually considered the "networks" (CBS, NBC, ABC, and recently Fox), used to be one of the biggest markets for feature films after theatrical release. But with increasing competition from cassettes, cable and syndication, network television has been declining rapidly through the 80's as a valuable market for movie exploitation.

So much more money can be made by producers and distributors from a rapid and widespread videocassette campaign that network "first-time-out-of-theaters" film events are all but disappearing. Whereas network broadcast in the past could represent up to 10% of a film's revenues, it has drifted down to 2–3% in most cases, and sometimes represents no share at all.

Syndicated Television. Syndicators used to be considered in the same category as "free television," but as methods of promotion and program sales grow more sophisticated, syndicated television has to be considered in its own right.

As the behemoth networks lean more and more toward mindless comedy and cop shows mixed with the occasionally "socially responsible" documentary or news report, syndicators have pulled off a number of coups with first-run movies and even originally produced mini-series for their customers (which can be re-edited for theatrical and/or video release in Europe).

Syndicators also have evolved many innovative economic incentives in exchange for airing rights having to do with selling or bartering sponsorship minutes, which an entrepreneurial producer can turn around and sell off at tremendous profits. The 90's should see a rapid growth in the power of syndicators to offer significant television revenues to independent producers.

As with so many of these categories, you can purchase published guidebooks listing syndicators, or you can call local television stations, ask for the programming director, and find out where he sees and/or acquires his shows.

Cable, Pay TV, Pay-Per-View (PPV). If anything, Cable TV grew even faster than VCRs in the last few years of the 80's—such is the desire for alternative programming to network fare. As communication technologies advance, the entire country is becoming wired for cable transmissions and only politico-geographic disputes remain in the way of every television-owning family having some sort of cable hook-up.

Cable companies are very secretive about what they pay for programming, and it has been theorized that they both outspend (in the area of first-run feature films) and underspend (in the area of "serious" documentaries or "art films") as compared with the networks.

For many years, cable channels primarily relied upon big theatrical movie coups, sports events, and concerts or variety shows not otherwise available to television viewers in order to differentiate themselves from free television. After all, if someone or a family is going to spend $20-50 per month, they had better consider that they're getting something special—and perhaps saving on video rentals and concert and sporting event tickets.

The critical statistic monitored by cable industry executives is "number of renewals per month." When it hovers at or drops below 50–75%, they get quite concerned. It has been predicted that cable groups would eventually have to produce their own original material at a quality and star-power level equal to or greater than the networks in order to survive.

One incentive for them to do so is the potential to turn that programming into subsequent theatrical and/or video release in Europe. The 90's should be the decisive period for the cable industry as a whole. If the Time-Warner Bros. merger is any signal (HBO, by far the largest and strongest of the cable channels, is owned by Time-Life), cable may be getting ready to generate very high profile products.

Since it is almost impossible to determine a meaningful average of what cable will pay for programs produced by independents, your best research method would be to watch cable shows, note the producers, and see if you can contact them directly. They may not want to share the results, but perhaps you'll find a fellow independent who'll tell all.

The real truth is probably that, thus far, the cable industry has no real economic standards. They'll pay what they consider they have to in order to provide the programming that their viewer surveys indicate is needed and wanted. Three million subscribers at $25 per month is a *huge* cash flow, and it is certainly worthwhile for a group like HBO to make sure they continue to get renewals.

If you did some intelligent cable viewer market surveys of your own on the desirability of your products, you might be in a strong negotiating position to get a meeting with a cable company's "Director of Acquisitions" or "Director of Programming."

The specialized instances of cable—Pay TV and Pay-Per-View—simultaneously excite and confound industry students. The CEO of one Hollywood mini-major predicted last year that Pay-Per-View will be the next giant revenue source for movies and other original programming. While he may be right, it remains to be seen if these niches can differentiate themselves in the public's mind sufficiently to get them to pay additional money every month, along with their basic cable rental.

Non-Theatrical. Before the days of the VCR boom, "non-theatrical" distribution accounted for 2–5% of a film's total revenues. Usually in 16mm print form, films would be sent to "captive audiences" at military bases, oil rigs, schools and colleges, airlines, prisons, cruise ships, etc., all of whom would pay flat rental fees for a screening. The popularity of videocassettes has further reduced non-theatrical film print distribution, which has been all but subsumed by its competitor.

However, some extremely low-budget avant-garde or "experimental" film productions can occasionally find enough of an audience at college film societies and art museums, especially if the maker is also invited to speak and is given an honorarium, that non-theatrical distribution could become worthwhile in specific instances.

UNUSUAL PRACTICES OF FILM DISTRIBUTORS

Before the Paramount Consent Decree, when the major production studios owned or controlled their own distributors and exhibitors, movies had a relatively direct and quick path to audiences. The theater manager would be given a release schedule from the distributor and book the film in at the agreed-upon time. His primary attention would be on keeping the projection equipment safe and functional, keeping the lobby and seats clean, and keeping the concessions fresh and plentiful.

After the Decree, exhibitors no longer had the certainty that the films sent over by the distributor would be of the quality to ensure an audience. To gain control over the exhibitor, distributors developed some business practices that ultimately swung the balance back to them despite the Decree.

91

Blind Bidding. A distributor will sometimes announce to potential exhibitors their slate of upcoming releases. Sometimes, these pictures haven't even been financed, let alone produced. Naturally, the distributors make them sound as appealing as possible, emphasizing anticipated stars in the cast and well-known and successful writers, producers and directors.

Also, if the genre is particularly topical or there is some other decidedly exploitable aspect to the picture, the distributor will discuss such in promotional flyers, "film market" displays, and through "teaser" videos or film clips. In effect, the distributor is trying to get a "bidding war" going amongst exhibitors for the right to show the picture.

This process of vying for a film without first having seen it is known as "blind bidding." Obviously, it can be a dangerous practice, since the movie may not live up to its promotional promise. The distributor's rationale, of course, is that if he can get an exhibition commitment, especially in the form of a cash advance, he can then use those funds to finance the picture's production, or he can borrow against them or use them as collateral for a letter of credit.

One Academy Award-winning director told me about a producer who offered a major star a $4 million fee to appear for three weeks in his current picture. The director expressed shock at the star's salary, and the producer said, "Watch this!" He proceeded for the next hour to telephone directly to the major distribution and exhibition chains throughout Europe to tell them of his upcoming product with the star. After the hour of calling, he had garnered $8 million in guaranteed cash advances. He turned to the astonished director and said, "See, I just ripped off 'star X' for $4 million."

Nonetheless, there have been enough box-office failures with major talent that exhibitors have become reluctant to offer distributors such cash advances unless there is some kind of rebate, or "escape clause," in case of poor performance.

In the 1970's, the practice of blind bidding put hundreds of individual theaters out of business. They had advanced all available and borrowable cash to some of the then-hot production companies (most of which went bankrupt in the 1980's), huge fees for the promise of showing the next hyped *Time* or *Newsweek* cover-story motion picture.

This practice became so pernicious that nearly half the states in America had exhibitor lobbies successfully entreat the local legislatures to pass laws against blind bidding. These are generally the smaller states, so the economic impact has not been huge. But it's still a hot and fearsome enough issue for producers and distributors that after one large New England state outlawed blind bidding in the mid-80's, several major studios took out full-page ads in the Hollywood trade papers vowing never to make pictures on location there again. (The state subsequently recanted, and itself now takes ads in the trades promoting film-making services available locally.)

Block Booking. Another practice arising out of the distributor's desire to wrest control back from the exhibitors subsequent to the Consent Decree, is "block booking." In this case, the distributor informs the exhibitor that if it wants to show "anticipated big Christmas hit 'X'" it will also have to show lesser films "Y" and "Z."

Again, exhibitors rebelled, and many states enacted measures outlawing block booking. In 1989, there was a significant legal case in one of the largest states that has outlawed the practice, and the courts found against the major distributor's local representative.

Interestingly, the major itself disclaimed any knowledge of its block booking tactics, and denied any complicity in the matter. The individual rep has been left to bear the brunt of the legal actions, suffering a fine and some disgrace. There is every indication that this individual possesses a large amount of potentially damaging information about normal distributor tactics in the area, and the industry awaits further developments in the matter.

Block booking can also be disadvantageous for the producer. If your film is "one of the block," especially the one without the big star, you can see how an unscrupulous distributor might attempt to charge off all the P&A and related costs, or at least larger than your fair share, of the total package to each individual film within it. Attempts to prove this kind of unfair practice are time-consuming and costly, and the best defense against it is to position yourself as a consistent supplier of excellent film product so that it would not be to anyone's benefit to cheat you now, lest you threaten to withhold your future films from that particular shady distributor.

Both blind bidding and block booking are unfortunate legacies of the Consent Decree. They are unusual business practices which give credence to something long suspected by producers— very few distributors or even major studios have certainty beyond "gut feel," or sequels to proven smash hits, as to what kinds of pictures audiences wish to see. So they look for any advantage over exhibitors they can get.

With financiers and producers controlling the creation and distributors controlling the release of product, they evidently consider that exhibitors will be forced to take any available films just to keep their doors open. Some industry analysts even think the major producers and distributors have attempted in the last few years to force out independents' access to movie theaters by booking films up to a year in advance, even with re-releases, and by threatening further withdrawal of product if the prime theater is not available during specified times.

If an independent cannot find a distributor to handle his single film because there's no apparent longevity or continuity to the relationship, or can't get a theater to show it because of prior commitments, then the giants are forcing out the small competitors—which is exactly the situation the Consent Decree was supposed to remedy.

However, in the somewhat relaxed business climate of the Reagan and post-Reagan eras, some exhibitors, distributors and producers are becoming involved together again, through mutual stock ownership if not direct sale or outright purchase. Interpretation of the Consent Decree is being pushed to the limit, and the 90's, no doubt, will be a turning point in one direction or the other.

There are many court cases pending as of this writing, and the film legal community anxiously awaits the outcomes.

In any business, when producers of a product do not have a guaranteed outlet to their publics, there are two choices: flood the market with the best possible product and trust that "quality will out," or restrict product so consumers will be forced to take what's available.

Output from the major studios over the past two decades has been anywhere from one-fifth to one-tenth what it was during the 30's and 40's. This is but one aberrated response to a governmental move to strive for greater competition in the marketplace, and may be why many independents, instead of trying to fight it out for domestic screen time with the majors, have opted for the newer markets of "made for video," cable, and other release formats.

Eventually, independent producers will stop considering what they might make from a hit in domestic theatrical release, and instead will come up with production budgets they are confident can be recouped from the ancillary markets.

Film distribution is a field ripe for innovative marketing techniques and unique release strategies. Producers are well advised to keep abreast of technological advances and coming exhibition trends.

As ever, the questions will be (a) how a project's budget should be determined, given the likely venues that will eventually flow money back to the producer; and (b) how to extract the most possible dollars from whatever markets *are* available.

BOOK THREE

EXHIBITION

EXHIBITION

Definition: *the showing of films to a public at a select place and time.*

Result: *the maximum number of satisfied paying customers spreading positive word-of-mouth.*

CHAPTER 6

EXHIBITION

P roducers cause films to be made and distributed to many markets; potentially the largest of these is movie theaters. Theater owners are called "exhibitors," and the public screening of films is called "exhibition." After the artistic and creative satisfaction of production, it is the results of exhibition that all filmmakers live by—audience acceptance, critical praise, revenues and, ultimately, the opportunity to make more films.

There are some interesting statistics which every producer

should know regarding public movie-going habits. First, until the 80's, the number of people going to movies had been declining steadily since the "Golden Age" of Hollywood major studio production. And although the gross revenues from theater admissions has been reaching all-time highs over the past few years, a large part of this is due to increased ticket prices.

The number of movie screens in the U.S. and Canada has ranged between approximately 25,000 and 30,000 over the past decade, and though the number continues to rise, this does not mean that many more theaters are being built—it means that older theaters are being converted into multi-plexes (anywhere from two to 18 screens per theater structure).

Of these screens, the best ones, as measured by quality of location, seating and equipment, generally are controlled by the major distributors. Independent distributors and producers often have to rely upon the "fringe" theaters and playdates.

Distributors separate theaters' locations into "key" and "non-key" cities. There are about 215 key cities, and their movie theaters can generate upwards of 75% of a major film's domestic theatrical revenues. These key cities also can be further separated by the average length of a successful film's run—2, 4, 6, 8, and 12 week towns.

ADVERTISING, PUBLICITY, PROMOTION

Exhibitors expect a film to be supported by *advertising (including trailers), publicity,* and *promotion.* These costs are usually borne by distributors and producers, though, as with all parts of the film business, they are highly negotiable areas.

It is vital for the independent producer to understand that these elements of a film's release are not luxuries, they are necessities. This is why distributors and exhibitors alike rarely consider a film's negative cost to be very significant in its own right. In other words, it is all too common for the producer and his investors to think that once a film recoups its production cost, they'll start seeing profits.

When you consider that an advertising budget alone can equal the production cost, you realize that getting the picture made is but half the battle. Recoupment of advertising and promotional costs is of even greater importance to the distributor and exhibitor because this represents cash directly out of their own pockets, along with all the indirect operating costs of establishing and maintaining a "machine" or network that can execute these campaigns and programs.

So the distributor and exhibitor, upon seeing a new picture, evaluate not only its absolute quality, but whether or not this is a project into which they want to become investors of a sort themselves. This, of course, ties into their ability to find or create an audience who is willing to pay the price of admission.

Generally, the more desirable a movie's component elements (cast, director, genre), the higher the percentage of advertising and promotional budgets which will be borne by a distributor and/or exhibitor. The less desirable a movie's elements (publicly unknown talent of unproven box-office appeal), then either a higher percentage of the advertising and promotional budgets must be borne by the producer, or those amounts will certainly be charged back to the producer by the distributor and/or exhibitor as a recoupable cost.

Though most distributors and exhibitors strive for and maintain a "standard" arrangement, the truth is that every picture must be considered on its own terms. Actually, if a producer can exact a sizable advance from either the distributor or exhibitor, he might not care what costs have to be recouped first before any profits are seen.

For one thing, he will have established a precedent, suggesting that he is capable of producing movies that are desirable enough to extract an advance. This will help him immensely on

101

negotiations for any subsequent project. Also, his production investors will see that quick returns *are* possible. And, finally, with the investors out of pocket for the entire production and postproduction period, it may be reasoned that some cash flow is better than none.

Notwithstanding the liabilities associated with accepting advances that do not equal the production costs, as mentioned in the chapter on distribution, it may be that if you've made a movie strong enough to extract an advance or a minimum guarantee from an exhibitor, you ought to take it. The word can spread through the distribution and exhibition industries that your pictures have a commercial appeal, and this can translate into a much easier time of production financing the next time out.

ADVERTISING

Advertising usually represents the largest expenditure during the life of a movie apart from its direct production cost. The campaign usually begins two or more weeks prior to a picture's opening. Depending on the nature of the release pattern, it can take the form of national television and radio spots, local television and radio spots, national magazines, newspapers, billboards, local magazines and flyers, and the preparation of trailers for showing in theaters.

The first purpose of advertising, of course, is to arouse interest in a film. The hope is that this interest will translate into box-office dollars. While advertising has never turned a poorly performing picture into a hot box-office attraction for any sustained period, it has brought people into the theaters for at least the first week or two.

From there, word-of-mouth seems to take over and become the most potent form of advertising, outdistancing all other uses of media. But the thrust of the first two weeks' performance is so significant in determining a film's future that producers, distributors and exhibitors have all shown willingness to support a film if there is any indication whatsoever that audiences will attend.

Advertising is one of the few areas of the film industry that utilizes market research and testing. Commonly, a distributor (sometimes in consultation with the producer and/or studio) will prepare more than one ad campaign, and then test them in similar representative towns around the country to determine the most effective marketing thrust.

If a film is not squarely in any one genre, but has, say, elements of adventure, romance, action and mystery, there might be a different ad campaign emphasizing each of these. Then, professional survey services will poll the early attendees and determine which of the audiences felt most satisfied.

With that information, a distributor might eliminate all the other ad campaigns assuming that the most satisfied audience will give the film the best word-of-mouth. If that word-of-mouth can be tied back into the ad thrust as well, it can enhance a picture's drawing power.

Producers are often so concerned about the nature of a film's advertising campaign that they will negotiate away other benefits (such as profit participation) in order to have a strong say in the content and style of the ads. This can go so far as to include a producer's input into ad copy and artwork, content of radio and TV spots, and editorial privileges over the clips utilized in trailers.

Every producer and every audience member has endured the discrepancies between a film's ads and the way it actually appears on screen. "Honesty in advertising" is a hot topic when it comes to the film industry. One thing is known with certainty—public word gets out fast, and while an exploitative but false impression of a picture can be generated in early advertising and can seem to be a way to drive audiences in, if the movie doesn't live up to the ad's promises, it will be shunned.

Sane advertising for a film should, in as exciting a way possible, give a direct and accurate indication of what the film is about and to what audiences it might appeal.

A classic advertising technique, seldom well-applied to movies, is "positioning." This is a method of comparing an unknown quantity to a known one. For films, it could be: *"This director/ movie out-Hitchcock's Hitchcock..."* The difficulty in applying this concept to film advertising is in choosing the correct comparison for the intended audience. You would have to carefully survey a representative sample of your anticipated public in order to make sure you're "hitting the right button."

For example, if you've made a romantic adventure film, are you better off comparing it to a well-known love story or action-adventure film? If you choose the wrong one, you may end up losing both audiences. If you try for a "crossover" audience, indicating in your ads that with your film they're getting the best of both genres, then you risk diluting the intense interest of either group.

Regardless of the overall advertising approach you choose, remember that exhibitors are often looked upon merely as landlords of screens, but in fact, they are one of the most valuable sources of information as to what constitutes a successful ad campaign for a given type of picture in a given neighborhood during a particular season. Experienced distributors and producers alike consult an exhibitor's knowledge and shape their advertising considering this input.

PUBLICITY

Publicity could be defined as those methods of increasing public awareness of a movie other than the paid forms of advertising mentioned above. This can include newspaper and magazine feature stories, television "news" and "magazine format" interviews, radio interviews and newsbreaks, public appearances by people associated with the production (actors, directors, producers), and other "media hype," ranging from fashion styles or innovative products shown in the film.

Publicity often commences even before a film is produced, and can continue through a picture's opening. Most films employ a *Unit Publicist* during shooting, sometimes even during prepro-duction, to plan and execute media and community publicity for a film.

The unit publicist works in concert with the producer's wishes and, if known, the intended distributor's style. Above all, the unit publicist's efforts should be geared toward enhancing public interest and awareness in the film such that by the time it's released, there's already an anxiously awaiting public. An exhibi-tor who is bidding for the rights to show a film will be favorably affected if there's already a "buzz" about the picture.

Famous examples of highly controlled publicity range back to the first *Star Wars*, where every single "leak" about the picture was dictated by George Lucas and the machine he had established during the more than two years of his picture's planning and production—all the way up to the recent *Batman*, and its intelligently-placed articles about the film's new look and the young director's unique vision and dark sense of humor.

An exhibitor, who will not really make money from a film unless it shows "legs" (remains popular or increases in popularity during the first few weeks), is as concerned about publicity for the movie as he is about its ad campaign. Some publicity tends to be self-congratulatory, and not really have an impact on a film's success. The best publicity takes into account the viewpoint of the potential audience and determines not what the stars or director and producer want to hear, but what will elicit the most public interest and anticipation.

One measure of effective film publicity is how many "column inches," or how much television and radio airtime, the picture receives. But the real statistic is: *how many people attend the film in the first two weeks*. Since the industry agrees that after that, it's mainly word-of-mouth that must carry a picture, it's clearly the job of publicity to drive sufficient numbers of people into the theater during that time so that if the picture speaks well to the intended audience, then it will have the success it deserves. Intelligent publicity can achieve something that no amount of paid advertising can.

PROMOTIONS

Promotions usually commence around the time of the advertising campaign, and often involve games, contests, giveaways, and the like. We've all seen the movie logos on the sides of fast-food soda cups, and as with *Batman*, hats and teeshirts well in advance of the film itself.

The great value of promotions is that they can get kids, the prime movie audience, excited about a picture and feeling they have to see it as soon as it's released. This ensures a big first-two-week audience, and can hearten a distributor and exhibitor. It also increases the likelihood that at least some of the filmgoers will give the picture positive word-of-mouth.

A distributor or exhibitor can entice a local or national vendor to pay for a significant part of the promotion by pointing out that every movie ad dollar and publicity article or report crosses over and promotes the product or vendor as well. Specially imprinted "Frisbees," sports and clothing items, mugs and cups, signed photos, and the like, can make the movie appear to be an already accepted part of daily life, adding to the audiences' desire to see the movie early.

Local restaurants and service companies can join in, and proudly boast of their participation in a movie's production. Since advertising is so expensive, it can be appealing to a manufacturer or service facility to, in essence, have their advertising paid for by the distributor and/or exhibitor in exchange for providing their product or service to a picture.

One independent production company in New York shoots all

its pictures in small towns in New Jersey. They send "advance men" to the town during preproduction to negotiate food, housing and other services (often including local labor as production assistants) with local vendors, in exchange for shots in the film that feature their establishments and products. The vendor also gets a credit at the end of the picture and is invited to have the staff appear as extras in the background of various scenes.

Airlines can fly stars around during a press campaign, or even the crew during production, in exchange for mention in a film's credits or ads. There are "product placement" brokers and agents who arrange elaborate "cross-promotions." Properly done, everyone benefits, since each ad dollar and column inch is doing at least double duty. But if poorly thought out—especially if the film itself does not measure up to expectations created by the promotion—the results can be ludicrous, and everyone involved can be sorry to have been associated with the picture.

Whether on a large studio scale or a modest independent scale, promotions can be mutually rewarding when the right amount of salesmanship is combined with sufficient publicity.

THE RELEASE

Since as much as 80–90% of a film's advertising budget will be spent during the first two weeks of its release, the exhibitors and distributors are extremely interested in an accurate reporting of these results. If the revenue stays the same or grows after the first week, the chances are the film has positive word-of-mouth and will be successful overall; there may be additional advertising backup to ensure that public interest remains high. If the revenues dip after the first week, the chances are that the word-of-mouth is poor, and advertising might be pulled back. So advertising is geared to attracting the largest possible segment of the target audience right away.

Because the largest percentage of a distributor's direct expense on a project (advertising and prints) occurs prior to and through the first two weeks of a film's exhibition, the distributor usually receives a huge percentage of these initial weeks' revenues. This can amount to as much as 90% of the box-office take.

After the film has established a successful run, the percentage slides rapidly—80-20, 70-30, and so on, until a 50-50 split or better is attained. On average it can be said that the exhibitor and distributor will split the proceeds roughly equally over time.

Box-office proceeds are only one source of revenues for a film exhibitor. Concessions—popcorn, sodas, etc.—can provide as much as 50% of a theater's profits, and they are not shared with distributors. So most exhibitors will develop a feel for what types of films draw what types of audiences, including their food-buying habits, and they'll gear their offerings accordingly. As an example, as the baby-boomers have grown up, we have seen espresso and cappucino bars appear inside lobbies that used only to have Coke, popcorn and candy bars!

In a 90-10 deal as mentioned above, the theater owner is naturally quite concerned lest the picture play only one or two weeks on a first-run. So an exhibitor might try to negotiate with a distributor that before the split occurs, he at least can recoup some of his weekly expenses, the house "nut" or "floor." If an exhibitor has operating costs (rent, equipment, personnel, etc.) of, say, $5,000 per week, he may be allowed to deduct that from box-office receipts prior to splitting 90-10 with the distributor.

If he doesn't get his nut covered due to a picture's poor performance, he can sometimes even get a consideration from the distributor by way of reduced terms; or, if he had advanced something to the distributor, he might even get a rebate. After all, the distributor has a vested interest in keeping theaters alive, and exhibitors have a vested interest in continuing to have a supply of movies.

The distribution-exhibition phase of the film business is interesting in that each side desperately needs the other, primarily a result of the enforced governmental split of the two functions. Yet they have historically been terribly afraid of one another.

Distributors frequently employ "counters" (people who mill about ticket booths and lobbies observing how many people enter) to ensure that exhibitors are not giving them a short count. And exhibitors have attempted to reduce the power of distributors by such methods as "product splitting."

In product splitting, various exhibitors will secretly agree not to bid against one another on competitive films in the hopes of driving the distributor's price and terms down. As with block booking and blind bidding, product splitting has been outlawed in a number of states.

It is interesting to note that that all of these unusual practices arose subsequent to the Consent Decree, in an effort to regain some control or predictability over the anticipated film revenues.

MARKET RESEARCH

Modern marketing researchers would claim that if producers, distributors and exhibitors really understood their audiences' needs and wants, then control would start with what kinds of films were made in the first place. However, film, more than any other business, has an almost paranoid view of marketing research. It is almost as though industry leaders fear learning that something can be known and understood about audience tastes. This is one of those areas where the art/business dichotomy crosses over.

Occasionally, an advertising or market research firm will test a few different ad campaigns once a film has been made. But virtually never does a producer or distributor attempt to survey in advance the prospective audiences to determine what they'd like to see.

The occasional daring producer will ask a simple question to someone standing in line: "What kind of film would you like to see?" The answer is invariably a socially acceptable answer: "Oh, one with lots of good things in it for the family." It might be much more useful to ask a moviegoer: "What film has anyone recommended to you lately?" or "Have you recommended any films lately to a friend?"

Because of the fear of over-standardization and/or "losing their magic," producers, distributors and exhibitors would sooner risk millions of dollars on a production than figure out the correct survey to find out what a potential film audience member would *really* like to see.

As marketing research becomes more and more a part of the business environment, though, the film industry will have to learn to adopt these techniques to their unique problems. There are now computerized databases at quite affordable prices available to any business. They offer in great detail the entertainment-dollar expenditures of the moviegoing public, including the usual lifestyle demographics, such as which magazines they read, what shopping malls they frequent, which days and nights of the week they reserve for leisure activities, and so on.

This should eventually translate into more intelligent film marketing campaigns. Independents, who have often made their films with a specific audience in mind, have in the past led the way with clever approaches to finding their public, and they should continue to do so.

CRITICS AND OTHER STRANGERS

This seemingly willful ignorance among the majors about audience preferences has allowed other forces to shape public opinion about a film. Critics for newspapers, magazines, television and radio have risen to huge prominence recently and, in some cases, their own brand of stardom.

It has never been proven that a significant percentage of potential filmgoers make their choice on the basis of what a critic says. On the other hand, each of the three tiers of the film industry pays attention to reviews and blurbs as a signpost of audience response.

Actually, in this environment, the producer can "play the critics" much as he can "play the financiers" or "play the distributors." In other words, he can seek out critics who had been favorable to his type of film in the past. Special previews, screenings, and press releases can be directed toward such a critic, and he can virtually be seduced into talking up the positive aspects of the picture.

While there are no reliable statistics regarding critics' impact on the potential audience, there is ample evidence regarding critics' influence on what films distributors and exhibitors continue to promote, regardless of initial box-office results.

If audiences are not patronizing a given film early on *and* the critics dislike it as well, then there is little hope that distributors and exhibitors will agree to continue playing the picture, even for the length of its initial contracted release. But if critics champion a film in spite of its poor initial box-office, there *is* some chance that distributors and exhibitors will alter and/or sustain a p.r. campaign to try to identify and drive the correct potential audience into the theaters.

Though film festivals used to be the "kiss of death" for potentially commercial pictures, distributors and exhibitors now attend them to scout for modest, undiscovered projects. In some cases, major studios that used to shun festivals have even been known to vie for the "premiere" slot at a festival in order to enhance the legitimacy of a project considered to need a specialized send-off before a wide public release.

There are many excellent guidebooks to film and video festivals around the world which list dates, entrance requirements, prizes (if any), and the kinds of films sought. Though rarely are there financial rewards, the exposure to critics and public at these events can be exploited by the marketing-conscious independent producer to create a groundswell of interest in his picture.

111

That interest can translate into a "bidding war," and has even led to major distribution and widespread exhibition. Also, as important as that exposure is the fact that if a producer comes to be known for high-profile films, this can ensure attention on future projects.

The important point here is that producers must be seen as continual sources of product; distributors must be known as being associated with innovative and creative producers; and exhibitors must have a steady flow of films to keep their doors open. Played right, this system can develop a synergy, and the relationships established now can provide a backbone for future success.

ALTERNATIVE MODES OF EXHBITION

One technique used by independents with more modest films is to treat both distributors and exhibitors as "rentable" services and facilities. If, prior to selling off any of the rights to his film, a producer can finance a picture fully, and even provide at least some of his own P&A funds, then he can approach distributors and offer to "rent" their services for a set weekly or monthly fee.

While it can be argued that a distributor will have less incentive for performance this way since he will not share in any profits, it is also true that the distributor would like to continue to get his weekly cash flow from the producer. Therefore, he'll endeavor to do, at minimum, an acceptable job.

Similarly, an independent can "four-wall" a picture. That is, he can rent theaters, one at a time or as a group, and cover the exhibitor's "nut," plus some. There again, the exhibitor won't profit beyond his fees, but at least he knows his rent is covered. Four-walling is especially applicable during off-seasons—such as after Christmas, or between Labor Day and the commencement of Thanksgiving, and the subsequent holiday season.

Four-walling is risky for the producer if he's renting the theater out of his own pocket, but on occasion it succeeds. The most famous example of this is *Billy Jack*, which started a mini-industry for its producer. Other well-known examples can be found in pre-Easter and pre-Christmas family-oriented documentary films, for which we see "saturation" advertising on television, announcing: *"This Week Only."*

There are numerous theories about the future of traditional film exhibition. While some analysts believe that the movie palaces are becoming dinosaurs due to the explosion of technology and new media, others think this is the perfect time for theaters to spruce up their appearance and comfort level to lure the ticket-buyer.

Also, High Definition Television (HDTV) and other new technologies will probably find their way into movie theaters in the near future.

Regardless of all these changes, the moviegoing experience will probably remain a special event for audiences everywhere. The educated independent filmmaker who is wise to the needs of each branch of the production-distribution-exhibition triad is in a strong position to provide films for tomorrow's audiences.

BOOK
FOUR

VIDEO

CHAPTER 7

VIDEO

VIDEO: ITS HISTORY AND FORMATS

In the early 1960's, a new technology for capturing and transmitting moving images was created—videotape. Videotape looks like, and is related to, the same kind of material that you find in audio tapes. A sheath of millions of fine metallic particles (kind of like metal sawdust) is bonded to a clear and flexible base. These particles can be magnetized, and when an electric current is passed through the tape as the tape rolls past a "magnetic recording head," the particles take on a new configuration from the random array that occurs when the tape is manufactured.

(When you play a blank fresh tape in your videocassette

117

recorder [VCR], you see "snow," or the electronic equivalent of randomly placed metallic particles.) When you hold magnetized videotape up to the light, you do not see images or frames as you do with film. It is opaque and does not look any different than the raw tape.

When visual information is broken down into an electric current and applied to a blank tape, the new configuration of metallic particles has now captured the images that had generated the current in the first place. When this new configuration is played back over a "playback head," the images appear on a video monitor or television set.

This remarkable technology has allowed the transformation of any moving visual information (such as feature films, documentaries, television shows, cartoons, etc.) into a form (the videocassette) that can be played on any home television set with the assistance of a VCR.

There are many formats in which videotapes can be produced and/or distributed. These include: 2-inch; 1-inch; ¾-inch; Betacam (high-speed ½-inch); Betamax (½-inch) I and II; Remax or M format (high-speed ½-inch); VHS (½-inch); Super VHS (½-inch); Super 8.

Also, a production shot in film can be transferred to any of these video formats, either after principal photography in order to prepare for editing and release, or after editing and initial theatrical exhibition to be suitable for subsequent home release.

Most theatrical pictures are produced in 35mm film; exhibited in 35mm or 70mm prints on initial release; reduced to 16mm for release in smaller theaters or during a second run; transferred to 1-inch videotape as a master from which VHS (Video Home System) copies are made for sale and rental in video stores. More than 80% of all videos are released in VHS for home consumption.

Projects produced in video are usually shot in 1-inch or Betacam; mastered to 1-inch; and distributed in VHS. For some years,

VHS and Betamax fought it out to become the favored home system, with VHS becoming utterly dominant by the mid-80's to the point where many video stores no longer even stock Betamax copies of popular films.

There are some video purists who maintain that Betamax is an inherently higher-quality system due to its somewhat greater image resolution deriving from its faster tape speed shuttling through the machine. However, Sony's initial decision to retain all rights to Betamax technology as opposed to JVC's decision to license out VHS technology doomed the former to a highly limited market.

Sony, though, with its professional quality Betacam (running at six times normal speed) has continued to be the dominant production medium for projects made in video.

PRODUCTION VS. RELEASE

Should you shoot in film or video? Most newcomers to these media think that budget is the primary criterion, assuming that video is always less expensive. This is untrue.

The most critical questions are: for what primary mode of exhibition are you intending your project, and what aesthetic criteria will you need to fulfill in order to suit your own standards or the expectations of the genre?

If you hope your main audience will be in movie theaters, with television and videocassettes as your secondary audience, then it is still virtually the world standard to produce your film on 35mm negative stock, usually manufactured by one of the three major world suppliers—Eastman Kodak, Fuji and Agfa-Gevaert.

Many directors and cinematographers have personal preferences among these three for aesthetic reasons. Often, these stocks will be tested in the production environment with its own unique light and atmospheric conditions in order to determine the most suitable color and light reproduction values for the project at

119

hand. The three stocks are very similar in price, and processing has identical costs, so producers rarely are concerned about the brand of raw film.

From time to time, there are budget-minded independent producers who attempt to make a theatrical film in 16mm and then blow it up to 35mm for theaters. The technology for this exists, and it is reasonably sophisticated. However, audiences *can* tell the difference, and the only projects which can successfully do this are ones where the mood of the piece is suitable to the grainier "moody" or "documentary" look offered by a 35mm print of a picture shot in 16mm.

Also, the blow-up process is costly, and so producers who consider this method solely as a cost-savings technique ought to confirm the budget impact on their particular movie with an experienced production manager and postproduction supervisor.

The general rule is: if your picture is going to be shown in a number of movie theaters around the world, it should be shot in 35mm film.

If your picture is going to have any video life after its theatrical release, then most likely a 1-inch "broadcast quality" master will be struck from a specially prepared "low-contrast" copy of your film, and this tape will be used as the duplication master for your video dubs.

80% or more of your video copies will be in the VHS ½-inch format, and the fact is that VHS copies look virtually the same whether the 1-inch had been struck from a 35mm print or a 16mm print. Therefore, if your film is not expected to have a theatrical life, it could be that 16mm will suffice as your production medium.

In the case of Movies of the Week or mini-series in television, these are often shot in 35mm since even though they'll only play on TV in the U.S., they well may have a theatrical life in Europe or elsewhere.

In the late 1980's, the thirst for movies intended only for video rental was so strong that a number of producers made pictures in the Super 8mm film medium (theretofore reserved for home movies or low-budget industrial films), and then transferred the material to a high-quality video master. Costs of entire feature films shot this way ranged from $10,000 to $50,000.

Audiences were apparently satisfied with the appearance of the finished product, as long as it also abided by the laws of its genre (horror, action, exploitation, etc.). The expansion of this particular market is anticipated to slow down in the 90's as audiences seem to want to have heard of the film through theatrical advertising before they're willing to rent it in the video shop. Therefore, the video store owner may decide not to stock the title unless he's heard of it himself, too.

As video technologies continue to improve (such as with the Betacam SP format), there is every chance that people will attempt to produce scripts directly on tape and bypass the film step altogether. Of course, this would have to apply primarily to projects intended only for home use, such as exercise and self-help videos, since there are currently very few large-scale exhibition facilities that are equipped to "project" videos.

However, another development for the 90's may be "movie theaters" equipped with HDTV playback units instead of film projectors. People who have seen this system work claim it is as good as or superior to a small neighborhood second-run theater showing a 16mm print.

In summary, most feature films will continue to be produced in 35mm film and then be made available in VHS video copies made from a tape master struck from the film. Most movies-of-the-week, mini-series, and major television series will be produced in 35mm film as well both for the quality of "the 35mm look" (fine grain, excellent color rendition, very clear image) and for the chance that they will be shown out of the U.S. in movie theaters.

Most documentaries will be shot on 16mm film (if any theatrical or film festival release is anticipated) or on tape, since audiences expect, and thus will accept, the grainier "grittier" look.

Finally, most projects made directly for video release where no theatrical release is intended will be shot directly on video. This includes exercise, self-help, promotional and marketing tapes and many other forms of informational programming. (The following chapter lists a number of these information categories.)

THE NATURE OF THE VIDEO MARKET

There has been much discussion both as to the nature of the impact of the home VCR on the production community as well as on the informational flows in society.

Whereas at first the VCR seemed destined primarily for industrial, corporate and scientific use, the decision of the Japanese manufacturers in the early 1980's to lower the price of each unit to under $500 was the turning point. In less than a decade, more than 70% of American homes with televisions have at least one VCR, and the number with two VCRs is steadily climbing.

By survey, the two major uses to which these machines are put are (1) delayed viewing of television programming; (2) playback of rented tapes. Up until the late 1980's, the majority of tapes shown in homes were rented only; because of price, very few, other than some self-help or exercise tapes, were purchased.

However, major suppliers of film and video product began lowering the price of feature films to $20 and under, and exercise and self-help tapes are often available as premiums along with the purchase of certain products. Therefore, it's anticipated that more and more tapes will be owned by viewers rather than just rented.

This implies that collections of tapes, just as personal book libraries, will become a fixture in the average VCR-owning home. Already, many public libraries have growing collections of popular and special interest videos and are allotting more and more of their annual purchase budgets to the acquisition of videos.

Even schools are beginning the transition from 16mm films to video for their audio-visual educational materials. According to surveys conducted by the world's largest distributor of informational films, Modern Talking Picture Service, whereas at the beginning of the 1980's 95% of schools favored 16mm film to video, by the end of the 80's, more than 50% owned VCRs and favored videos.

In fact, in the early 1990's, PBS, the Public Broadcasting System in the U.S., plans to install in-classroom video programming to an enormous number of junior high and high schools around the country.

As the society continues the transition from the industrial age to the information age, a growing amount of that information will be transmitted visually. Producers of video product, especially high-quality informational programming, have a virtually unlimited market for the future. Traditional narrative feature films will become but one of many video forms of great commercial appeal.

Elements such as packaging, marketing, and accompanying study guides and other materials, will also grow evermore important in establishing the leading producers. Except for access to production funds, independents have every bit as much opportunity as the majors to grab hold of this exploding field.

HOME VIDEO

Just as there has been a fundamental failure on the part of many producers to differentiate exactly the benefits and liabilities—economic, technical and aesthetic—of video vs. film as a production medium, there has been very little thought given to the unique capabilities of the VCR to introduce an entirely new kind of programming to the world-wide television scene.

For the first decade of VCR availability, most programming was constituted out of movies converted to videotape or somewhat high-brow documentaries normally associated with "PBS"-type specials. Even though viewer surveys continually indicated that VCR owners wanted material not otherwise accessible to them through movie theaters or on TV, very little original "made-for-home" programming occurred until the breakthrough *Jane Fonda Workout* tapes.

The startling million-plus unit sales at a high wholesale (39.95–59.95) and retail (59.95–79.95) price caused the entire production industry to turn around and begin to create material that met the apparent new requirements.

As it turned out, the Fonda tapes became a model for many of the new made-for-home projects. The elements common to these tapes included: (a) the presence of a celebrity; (b) a motivational "you can do it" theme; (c) fitness or "self-help" subject matter; (d) material not available elsewhere; (e) suitable for viewing in the household rooms most likely to have a VCR—bedroom and den/living room. While not every made-for-home tape has all these elements, most of the successful ones have at least a majority of them.

Two other factors have arisen toward the end of the 80's: (f) participation of a sponsor (a product or corporation); (g) built-in distribution network (the sponsor's existing distribution network for his prime product or service—catalogs, showrooms, mail order, etc.). A brief examination of these points may reveal something about the future trends in the field.

CELEBRITY

The presence of a celebrity in a "made-for" has proven to be nearly mandatory if you're seeking some sort of outside sponsorship of a tape. For example, if you're making a video about some health or exercise topic, the chances are that there will be an opportunity to show and utilize a product or a piece of equipment.

This has led many producers of such tapes to contact manufacturers or distributors of the product and offer to include their equipment in the video in exchange for a credit, production funds, promotional funds, and, perhaps, utilization of their normal equipment distribution channels to promote the tape. Very often, such a firm will already have some celebrities under contract or retainer representing their line of goods, and will negotiate with the producer to engage that individual to star in the tape.

In spite of the great success of the Fonda series of exercise tapes, there have been enough examples of poorly performing video releases starring a celebrity that the industry is no longer so sure of the absolute wisdom of hiring a high-priced star to host every tape.

Certainly, as with the star system in movies, it's one way to attract an audience, but unless the particular celebrity has been associated in the past with the tape's topic and thus considered some kind of an authority, or has such a huge absolute following as to guarantee patronage of *any* product they're associated with, then there's no guarantee that their participation will result in a payoff.

It may be that within any tape subject, there would be some celebrities that could be determined by survey who would definitely enhance the sales efforts. One idea that has recently been utilized is to combine a celebrity with a personal interest in the area along with a bona fide expert from the field. This, then, speaks to at least three audiences (celebrity's, expert's, the field's) and, hopefully, the synergy will create a fourth audience dedicated to the specific tape.

Another issue in employing a celebrity to host a home video has to do with his or her fees. There are athletes and movie stars who have commanded enormous salaries and profit participations for one or two days' work. These amounts can be so high that the producers virtually have no hope of recouping their costs from tape sales... *unless* they, too, write themselves into the production budget for a large fee and accept that this is all they will see from the video's proceeds.

This method conceivably could work if the tape's sponsor is using the project primarily as a promotion rather than as a profit center in its own right.

The producer might also be able to negotiate to become the tape manufacturer and packager, providing copies to the sponsor at an agreed-upon unit price. A producer who has established relationships with the major video dubbing houses by ensuring them numerous productions each year can arrange a very low per unit price for himself (1.50–3.50 per tape) and then mark it up two to four times and still deliver the copies to the sponsor at a price as good as the sponsor could negotiate for himself on a one-project basis.

Recently, a number of entrepreneurial producers have offered celebrities a huge percentage of the profits from a video (as much as 50%) in exchange for their taking a minimum up-front fee. This brings the entire production cost into a more manageable realm, and, for the short amount of time these tapes usually take to produce, can be lucrative as well for the star.

For reasons discussed below in "Collections," it may be significantly easier to realize profits on a home video project than on a feature film.

It's important to note that many successful tapes have *not* featured a celebrity host or participant. However, such projects usually either have the presence of one or more acknowledged authorities from the field (for example, the Jacques Cousteau tapes), or the producing entity itself has tremendous public identification as being a leader in the area (the National Geographic specials).

MOTIVATIONAL THEME

It has long been considered that one reason people go to movies is to be shown alternatives to their own lifestyles, and to be shown people struggling against odds to achieve their goals. It's almost as though the medium has a rehabilitative power. In spite of this, many movies also dwell on the darker sides of life and offer "downer" messages. Some of these films achieve critical acclaim and, occasionally, a significant public following. It may be that the viewer feels a sympathy or commiseration with the fates befalling the characters.

However, thus far, nearly every successful made-for-home video either has a purely entertaining function (concert films, sport events) or has a highly motivational theme. It's not mysterious that a majority of video titles carry a "you can do it/you can improve your life" theme.

Naturally, the fields of exercise, sports instruction, self-defense, diet, fashion, makeup, hairstyling and most other self-help topics have generated a vast array of titles for the home video market. It's almost as if people, in the privacy of their homes, are willing to admit that they'd like to improve their lives or they'd like to learn more about the world. The potential for playing and replaying a tape under circumstances of their own choosing seems to be a driving force in determining successful home video titles.

So wise video producers ensure that in their selection of topics they are offering material that will merit multiple viewings (aerobics and any sports instruction, cooking, etc.) and will encourage the viewer to await sequels and other follow-ups.

For example, surveys have indicated that if someone is, say, a golfer, and purchases one golf instruction tape, he is likely to purchase another. One highly successful producer of such tapes has said that a golfer will buy a tape if he believes that it will lower his score by just one stroke. For this reason, golf and other instructional tapes are often issued in series, each episode covering one specific topic. This creates a built-in audience for extensions of the series, and, if the tapes are sold via mail order, derives a remarkably valuable mailing list for any future videos or other related products, such as books and magazines.

Also, since golf, tennis and other sports have many allied fields (publications, clothing, equipment, public events), these are perfect tapes for promotional tie-ins.

As the home video market continues to develop, any kind of entertainment, therapy, or other leisure-time activity should prove to be a perfect field in which to issue a regular series of tapes. Some producers have even developed a subscription-based following, almost like a "book-of-the-month" club which, of course, drastically reduces production costs per tape since they'll shoot the whole series at one time and then release the shows periodically.

The great success of many aerobics tapes, in addition to the Fonda series, parallels the rise of health-club memberships and diet fads. Someone who is interested in the field will try most anything if it offers an opportunity for self-improvement. At first, there's usually a spurt of benefit, and then the results flatten off. However, having bought one such tape automatically creates an interest in subsequent similar tapes if the new ones have any claim at legitimacy (which is, as with movies, determined by critical response and word-of-mouth).

FITNESS AND SELF-HELP

As stated in the section above, any tapes that offer the viewer opportunity for education, training and enhancement of some aspect of his or her life can be a viable project for the producer. In addition to the participation of celebrities or experts, marketing becomes a key element in determining the tape's success. Since physical fitness and therapies of all kinds are currently enjoying a marketing boom, especially in the U.S., these make ripe fields for home videos. Many people are still shy to go public with their concerns for betterment (of themselves, their relationships, the environment, their spiritual lives, etc.), so the privacy factor in home viewing is paramount.

The concept of "interactive videos," tapes that cause you to *do things* while watching them, will be an ever-growing part of the home market. In fact, there are a number of educational experiments underway, including the PBS establishment of in-classroom programming for schools, that indicate the visual medium will be more and more relied upon to provide the stimulus and motivation necessary for real learning to take place.

Even corporations appear to be growing more aware of the need for a responsible commitment to quality video materials as a way of combating the rampant illiteracy and drug culture beset-ting us. Educational leaders around the country, such as Jaime Escalante, the phenomenal math teacher at East Los Angeles' Garfield High and subject of the film *Stand and Deliver*, are committing their teaching techniques to video in order not only to help students, but to demonstrate their successful methods for other teachers.

In fact, Escalante's new series, *Futures*, has been designed by the producers for broadcast, in-classroom "narrowcast," and home video release, as this is the only way they can fully reach their intended audience—secondary school students.

Video, in addition to being a major potential profit center for intelligent producers of programming, represents significant hope for improvement of education internationally.

EXCLUSIVITY

While feature films have been the mainstay of the home video market to date, we are fast approaching the state of "no more titles." In other words, a majority of the available classic films have already been transferred to video, and new releases are going to video as soon as contractually possible. So producers are increas-ingly thinking of original programming for home video (as well as cable TV) as an important element of their production activities.

The conventional wisdom is that if programming is available only in one medium, such as purchase for home VCR use, and if it's desirable (or made so through marketing), then there should be a certain predictable market for it. Moreover, if even within that market, the tape is only available through purchasing a specific product or service, then there is an even more likely customer base.

For example, one recent sponsored golf video was available for free if you purchased a set of the manufacturer's golf clubs. The video was available at half price if you purchased a dozen of their golf balls. And it wasn't available otherwise. Predictably, club and ball sales rose. When the rise leveled off, the tape was made available retail at pro shops and through magazines. Now, everyone who wanted the tape but didn't want clubs and balls had their chance, and the tape itself became a profit center.

Magazines and newspapers have created and offered tapes available only if you become a subscriber or if you renew your subscription. One publisher of an expensive quarterly technical business journal produced an even more expensive video newsletter, sent to journal subscribers at a discount and two weeks ahead of its being available on the open market. Magazine subscriptions soared, and, when word spread of the "scoops" in the video, tape sales boomed as well.

When production costs are kept within reason as compared with the projected increase in readership, a custom-made video can be a high-profile promotion and a profit center in its own right.

Exclusivity has always been a substantial marketing "button," and when combined with knowledge of a particular public's needs and desires, can be utilized effectively by the independent and entrepreneurial producer.

VIEWING LOCATION

Though a seemingly minor point, tape sales have been highest when the subject matter is conducive to viewing in rooms in a house most likely to have a VCR. Bedrooms, living rooms and dens have traditionally been the locations of the family VCR, alongside the family television. It is easy to see how entertainment and physical fitness tapes have fit into this pattern.

This also explains why food and cooking tapes have so far been less successful than anticipated. While many kitchens have small TVs, few have VCRs. This will change as more television households acquire multiple video players.

Along with the nationwide growth in "business hotels," VCRs are becoming available at a growing rate in hotel rooms. In addition to the usual movies and "adult entertainment," special interest programming such as local business, industry and shopping guides is proliferating.

SPONSORS

Though made-for-home videos have decidedly lower budgets than most feature films, they still require significant amounts of production funds. It's not uncommon for a 30–60 minute program to cost $50,000–250,000 or more, especially if a high-priced celebrity is involved. The medium is still new enough that predictable sales levels are hard to come by.

So independent producers are always looking for ways to offset their cash commitment. One of the best of these is to identify a sponsor for the tape who might have a vested interest in its success.

Typically, a corporation with a product or service that needs promotion makes a likely target. The corporation will usually have a v.p. in charge of marketing or public affairs who has an operating budget that could sustain the price of such a video. The executive will evaluate the potential investment in a tape alongside more traditional forms of advertising, primarily print ads and brochures. He will look at "cost per thousand" so that he can estimate just what his expenditure is to reach one current or new customer.

Factored into this absolute cost, however, will be the fact that videos command attention and have prestige associated with them in ways that print ads do not.

Furthermore, it has been proven that videos have a very high "pass-along" rate. In other words, a promotional video that contains entertaining or educational material will likely be given or lent to friends, neighbors and business associates in ways that magazines are not. Also, a video usually becomes part of a personal or office library, whereas magazines are tossed out weekly.

One difficulty in locating acceptable sponsors for a video is that many companies regulate their promotional budgets more than a year in advance, and do so via an advertising agency. Agencies are notoriously covetous of their clients and of their traditional approaches to the clients' campaigns. Some agencies even have installed their own video units, and bypassing these in a direct approach to the corporation can be almost impossible.

However, many companies do maintain special divisions with discretionary funds that must be spent each year apart from their usual advertising. Becoming familiar in advance with a corporation's ad, marketing and promotional patterns by reading their annual reports and corporate profiles (available from most large stock brokerages and in library business guidebooks) is an important piece of research prior to your direct pitch.

Many large companies even establish foundations dedicated to spending a predetermined annual amount of money. If the foundation can see how your proposed tape project might benefit them in terms of local or national goodwill, not to mention product sales, they may seriously consider investing in your video.

The entrepreneurial producer can negotiate to maintain some kind of ownership of the tape subsequent to the company's primary window of use (usually a year from first release). As direct profit from the tape is not usually the main goal of the sponsor, they're usually quite happy to relinquish exclusive distribution rights as long as they know you will at least keep the video promoted and in circulation.

Another significant benefit of corporate sponsorship is the opportunity for "cross-promotion." A publisher might release a videotape promoting a new book with the tape packaging even containing a discount coupon for book purchase. Similarly, the book might contain a tear-out card promoting the tape. Also, two companies, say a clothing manufacturer and a make-up firm, may realize that they can get double mileage out of co-sponsoring a topical video. Each promotes the other at half the normal cost and twice the exposure.

BUILT-IN DISTRIBUTION

As with feature films, distribution is a major element in determining a tape's success. The tape must be available at an affordable cost to the target audience.

Most video stores stock mainly the most recent movies, some classic movies, cartoons and other kids' programming, and a few special interest items. Their precious shelf space is rarely given over to the huge number of self-help and other informational titles. 10,000 units nationwide might be small stuff for movies that now deal in hundreds of thousands and sometimes millions of units, even if it could mean large cash flow to the independent producer and ample publicity for the sponsor.

So it is very appealing for a producer to link up with a company that already has a built-in distribution network for its products. For example, a make-up, hair or fashion tape can go right to the wholesalers and retailers who already stock the product line. All that really has to happen is for the buyer to become aware of the tape's existence and its likely boost to customer interest and sales.

Some companies develop an incentive program, giving their salespeople a certain number of tapes for free if they boost their product sales beyond prior levels. If they fail to do that, they still can buy any number of tapes they wish at a wholesale cost and then use the tapes as they see fit (lend them to customers, sell them, rent them, give them away as a promotion, etc.).

MODES OF DISTRIBUTION

There are a variety of ways videotapes are distributed. Nearly all methods differ from film distribution in one key aspect: the tapes are sold rather than licensed, so royalties are generally unavailable to the production team.

In other words, if you make a film or video which ends up being distributed in video, you sell copies to a videotape dealer. The dealer then can sell it himself and keep any profits, or he can rent it any number of times and keep all the proceeds, or he can give it away as a premium for the purchase of some other item.

This principle is known as the *"first sale doctrine"* and states that once the buyer has purchased the item he can do anything with it he wishes, as long as he does not duplicate it (which would violate the copyrights).

Though many producers are rebelling against this system, it is unlikely there will be a change in the near future. If for no other reason, policing the number of rentals would be a formidable task, not easily achieved. (Some inventors are trying to come up with a built-in "tape play" counter on a VHS plastic shell, but this so far has been unworkable on a broad scale.)

So from a producer's standpoint, he is interested in selling the maximum number of copies of his video. From the retailer's standpoint, he is interested in renting each copy he owns the maximum number of times.

Here is a typical scenario for a feature film producer: The producer finances and produces a movie and attempts to arrange for theatrical distribution and exhibition. In negotiating these rights, he usually sells or licenses the video rights as well.

This means that the distributor makes a high quality video master (usually in 1-inch tape from a low-contrast film print) and has a duplication house make numerous copies for sale to a video wholesaler (which may be a unit within its own company). Usual numbers range from 10,000 to hundreds of thousands to, occasionally, millions.

The distribution company or wholesaler then sells these copies to video retailers, which can include video stores (national chains or local "mom and pop" stores), department stores, convenience stores and markets, and special interest shops (sporting goods stores, high tech shops, fashion and beauty supply shops, etc.).

The wholesale price to these outlets is usually 70–90% of the eventual retail price. Every outlet attempts to set its own policy as to how many copies of each title it buys.

Since shelf space is the most valuable commodity the store has, it evaluates whether in a given instance it's better to stack up numerous copies of "hit" titles so it can maximize its immediate rentals (known as "depth of copy"), or whether it is better off spreading its resources over many varied titles ensuring the widest spread of renting publics. Smaller stores tend toward the former, and a few of the larger chains (such as Videotheque in Southern California) have become known as suppliers of exotic titles (foreign films, self-help and other special interest videos), along with the usual box-office hits.

Given the relatively high wholesale price on these tapes, only a low markup is possible if the tapes were intended for sale. So most stores concentrate on rentals since this maximizes their cash flow and keeps the tapes circulating. When the rentals die down for a particular title, the store often will sell the used copies at a substantial discount from even the wholesale price in order to make room for the new titles. In the meantime, all the producer ever has seen is the proceeds from the first sale to the wholesaler.

In the late 1980's, major suppliers of feature film video product tried several pricing levels—79.95; 59.95; 39.95; 29.95; 19.95; 14.95; etc. Sure enough, the lower the price, the more copies were sold. But since the duplication costs remained constant, the lower the price to the wholesaler, the more copies *had* to be sold to maintain the same profit margin.

Overall, the difference in profit results at each price level appeared to be trivial, and many suppliers ended up deciding that price was not nearly as important a variable as popularity of the title (which was determined by marketing and promotion).

And as demonstrated by the famous *Top Gun* example featuring a commercial at the head of each tape, promotional fees from sponsors could offset duplication costs and the tapes could be sold at much lower prices.

It appears doubtful, though, that major national corporations will want to participate in tape sponsorships in any but the most popular hit films.

Here is a typical scenario for the "made-for-home" informational, self-help or other special interest video: The producer determines a need by a public for a specific subject or title. He locates a distribution avenue, such as catalog sales (Sharper Image, Neiman-Marcus, or other chain of department stores, bookshops, etc.), special interest shops, direct sales through carefully placed ads in magazines, or following the existing network of a particular manufacturer or supplier of a good or service.

He then approaches a celebrity or expert in the field and extracts a commitment for hosting or "guest appearance" participation. With the anticipated distribution avenue and celebrity commitment in place, he finally approaches a potential sponsor who will either put up all or partial production funds or at least promotional funds in exchange for the exposure the tape will allow.

The producer then profits from duplication and packaging fees, possibly from a percentage of the sales (unless the tape is a give-away premium for the sponsor), and eventually from the reversion of rights to the producer after the sponsor has exacted his intended use.

Without any of these elements in place, the well-meaning producer who has made his "pet project" video may well end up with a garage or storage locker full of tapes.

COLLECTIONS

Collections of tape sale proceeds can be an easier job than with theatrical distribution fees. "Number of tapes duplicated," "number of tapes shipped," "net sales less returns" all should be fairly simple statistics to compile. And if you're engaging in direct sales via catalogs or magazine and television ads, you will know daily about orders and fulfillments. In fact, many magazines offer a "trade-out" service: free ad space in exchange for a percentage of all videos sold via the magazine. These numbers can be tracked without difficulty if you're also the supplier of the tapes.

The main difficulty in collections comes when you deal with a third party video distributor who may have an unknown "returns policy." Some distributors allow for 100% return rights by a retailer if he cannot sell the copies he ordered (or were foisted upon him by an overzealous distributor desirous of reporting high "tapes shipped" numbers for trade magazine statistics).

Others have a "no returns" policy, which usually results in fewer tapes shipped, thus fewer sales. Some have a "returns for exchange" policy where a vendor may return unsold tapes, but then must acquire an equal number of a comparable title in the distributor's catalog.

As with books and records, what you want to avoid is a situation where the distributor is always needing your next title in order to get the funds to pay you for the sales of your prior title. For this reason, many producers of made-for-home video product set up their own distribution machine and hope eventually to end up with a catalog of their own titles. This way, every promotional and ad dollar is marketing a series of tapes and the "per tape" cost is reduced.

To fulfill orders, which includes duplication, packaging, shrink-wrapping, and shipping, requires a small but persistent staff, and it's as easy to do this for a number of videos as for one. Plus you're in charge of your own collections.

PIRACY

The unauthorized duplication and sale of tapes is known as "piracy," and is a situation rampant in the video industry.

There are several extant technologies which can encode tapes with an electronic signal that renders them uncopyable. Even the FBI is actively involved in developing new tape protection procedures. However, all such methods have proven faulty, in that if the signal is strong enough to prevent copying, it can sometimes render a flawed playback, especially with an old or dirty VCR. If the signal is weakened to ensure better playback at home, then the tape can sometimes be duped with good enough equipment. The 90's should yield much more sophisticated protective technologies.

THE FUTURE

There are over 60,000 video titles currently available, and the number will grow by up to 10,000 per year. But there are probably over 100,000,000 VCRs in the U.S. alone, and as schools and institutions rely more and more upon videos as sources of reliable information and educational materials, there's every reason to believe that the producer of high-quality titles will continue to find markets for his work.

Since videos are now positioned not just as weekend entertainment but as valuable personal possessions, they will be collected as are books (or used to be). The entrepreneurial producer will be able to take advantage of this thirst for new and unique programming in the "Information Age." A knowledge of promotion and marketing will become the critical variable in determining your success in this field.

BASIC VIDEO FORMS

For the beginning video producer, there are numerous types of programs he can make before venturing into the costly and risky feature arena. They can provide a good experience base, and establish valuable corporate and other business ties which can be utilized as he ventures further into the "made-for-home" field. Here is a list of these formats:

1. The Corporate Image
2. Marketing
3. The Video Annual Report
4. The Sponsored Film/Video
5. The Electronic Press Kit
6. Fund-Raisers
7. Point-of-Sale
8. Training
9. Internal Communications
10. The Info-Mercial
11. Community Relations
12. Public Service Announcement (PSA)
13. Special Purpose Films and Videos

1. The Corporate Image

Description: Presents an overall image of a group, usually tailored to speak to the expectations of a specific audience. Incorporates effective, carefully selected and produced interviews, documentary footage, and graphics.

The graphics portion must embody the image or corporate "position" which the film/video is trying to enhance or modify. For example, the corporate logo can be presented dynamically; performance charts can "grow" or be "revealed"; various company products/services can be illustrated.

Running Time: 6–12 minutes.

Primary Uses: Special events such as conventions, trade shows, board meetings, stockholder meetings. Can be used for special mailings to accompany an annual report, or for direct mailings to targeted audiences.

Major Benefits: The most modern "positioning" tool. Features key members of the group, so adds the "personalized" touch, so important for today's businesses. Short form makes an impact on the audience. A strong identity is established or re-established.

2. Marketing

Description: A promotional item, usually aiding the sale of a specific product, idea, concept or service. It can be product-specific, generic, or modular. The modular form would include a short generic statement about the general field or industry, as well as a changeable section detailing some specific topic.

Running Time: 3–12 minutes.

Primary Uses: Used by salespeople as a promotional and explanatory tool for point-of-sale support in a controlled manner. Especially valuable in a group utilizing various levels and networks of distribution and dissemination.

Major Benefits: Perfectly controlled sales message, both in-person (point-of-sale) and through the mails. Very effective and efficient use of time. Can save on travel and entertainment expenses by isolating hot prospects from warm or cool leads. Can have follow-up programs and be used as a survey tool.

3. The Video Annual Report

Description: Once the exclusive domain of print media, this video genre is becoming highly popular among "leading edge" corporations. Similar to the "Corporate Image" format, there is an emphasis on annual performance, with facts and figures presented graphically and dynamically.

Running Time: 5–15 minutes.

Primary Uses: Same as printed Annual Reports. Suitable for mailings. Can be made available to libraries, universities, stock brokers, banks, etc.

Major Benefits: Can be more cost-effective and higher impact than high-gloss printed reports. Will be looked at and passed along more than written materials. Has a "pride of ownership" factor greater than print. Can even be personalized with the use of a video "character generator."

4. *The Sponsored Film/Video*

Description: Usually a documentary. Often about a topic loosely related to the sponsoring group. Contains hard information along with some educational, inspirational or provocative content. (Poor versions of this form have been called "propaganda," while excellent versions can be looked upon as truly valuable contributions to the society and culture.) Often of award-winning caliber.

Running Time: 20–30 minutes.

Primary Uses: Suitable for schools, colleges, various adult organizations, church and other community groups. If of sufficient quality, can also be broadcast on television or cable. Can gain videocassette or film print distribution as well.

Major Benefits: Because of its topical nature, the sponsored project can gain an enormous audience. The sponsoring group will be positioned in the viewer's mind with the subject or the viewpoint of the film. (Example: one major oil company sponsored a series of films about the Constitution and the Founding Fathers. The film became part of grade-school curricula.)

5. *The Electronic Press Kit*

Description: The video version of a press release. The producer provides his own video clips to television or other media. Can be presented as a "reportage" or just as "shots." Portions can be "lifted" for television, or the entire piece can be presented.

Running Time: Up to 5 minutes, with 15–90 second "lifts."

Primary Uses: A group or individual sends his own media kit ready for broadcast or other scrutiny. Can ensure more air time for your subject and your viewpoint.

Major Benefits: The producer can control what images are presented of his topic. If a "hard-to-get" subject, this can be quite valuable to the media. You can also include the desired historical material which a television or media department can't find or doesn't have time to locate. Makes information more accessible and easier to use for the media.

6. Fund-raisers

Description: The fund-raising film/video is a relatively recent, but already "classic" form. States the goal and purpose of the sponsoring group and lets its constituency know exactly what's needed to achieve it. Often utilizes celebrities or other opinion leaders as spokespersons who are members of or sympathetic to the group. Usually very stirring and emotional. Must be produced with excellent taste and a real understanding of the orientation of the viewing public.

Running Time: 5–15 minutes.

Primary Uses: Can be mailed out to previous supporters or new mailing lists. Can be utilized on its own, or in conjunction with a "live" event. Can introduce speakers or topics.

Major Benefits: Makes a direct emotional appeal for your cause. Provides immediate feedback. Can use well-known individuals in action supporting your group. Effectiveness overcomes cost.

7. Point-of-Sale

Description: Like a "long commercial" on a loop for continuous play at a specific site. Usually quite dynamic visually. Combines excellent and appealing imagery with choice bits of information.

Running Time: 1–5 minutes.

Primary Uses: Usually played on a VCR mounted in a special display, called a "kiosk," scattered throughout a store, or on sales counters on a portable VCR.

Major Benefits: Attracts a lot of foot traffic when in a public setting; very "upscale" presentation in a one-on-one situation. Makes a salesperson's job easier by highlighting in a codified way the key selling points of the product or service.

8. Training

Description: Trains someone in a specific skill, overall attitude, or general orientation toward a subject or concept. Can be straight exposition, or "interactive" if utilizing video or disc. Often is keyed to printed materials (workbooks, manuals, reports, etc.).

Running Time: Depends on written materials, study periods, etc., but is usually 20–30 minutes.

Primary Uses: Presents technical and conceptual information to staff, new members and other recruits, people shifting position within the group, transfers from other branches, consultants, and the like.

Major Benefits: Standardizes the message and manner of presentation. Individuals can work at their own speed. Saves "burned-out" lecturers. Allows for study "supervision" rather than "instruction." Can speak to various levels within a group, including executive, middle management or basic staff.

9. Internal Communications

Description: An announcement or other message, informational or inspirational, from one member of a group to another. Can include Presidential or other management and divisional reports.

Running Time: 2–60 minutes.

Primary Uses: Someone or a group needs to get a specific message to someone else or some other group. Managers report to seniors. Workers report to managers. One branch reports to another or to management. Can be recycled, added to, or otherwise modified.

Major Benefits: Provides current and "high tech/high touch" viewpoints to individuals within a group. Standardizes the message, and ensures that all personnel encounter the exact material without rumor or hearsay. Prevents "interpretation" beyond what is there for all to see.

10. The Info-mercial

Description: Resembles a news or talk show, but is actually an overt pitch for a product or service. Often has a neutral-seeming host who is quite well-prepared for the vital points that need to emerge. This format is made possible by "leased access" and other private or semi-private cable and satellite systems.

Running Time: 10–30 minutes.

Primary Uses: Excellent for informing a general public and/or creating actual leads through an "800" number.

Major Benefits: Appears to be a formal presentation by a third party. "Positioning" as "news" or "information" can make it seem something other than a commercial.

11. Community Relations

Description: This form speaks to specific publics and often is concerned with a topical or local issue. In long form, it would be called a documentary. In short form, it is called a Public Service Announcement (PSA). A classic public relations tool.

Running Time: 1–5 minutes or 15–30 minutes.

Primary Uses: Suitable for small local showings, large theatrical presentations, or cable, public access and even syndicated and network exhibitions.

Major Benefits: If used at the beginning of a campaign or program, it can smooth the way and answer questions or objections. If used during or subsequent to a situation or problem, it can handle ruffled feathers.

12. Public Service Announcement (PSA)

Description: Traditionally, a short-form commercial spot "in the public interest." Airtime provided by government edict. Often hard-hitting for dramatic impact, or one specific bit of information is driven home.

Running Time: 15–120 seconds.

Primary Uses: Some form of television broadcast.

Major Benefits: The sponsor of the PSA benefits by association with the topic at hand.

13. Special Purpose Films and Videos

This is the generic catch-all category covering anything not mentioned above. It can be designed for a special purpose, for a special audience, for special results. Perfect for "one-time" presentations to a specific group or individual. It probably should be accompanied by a survey or some other followup to see: how well did it work?

CONCLUSION

THE PARTING SHOT

This exploration of the modern marketplace for films and videos has been driven by a single idea: You can achieve your goals *if* you are informed about the economic realities of these mediums.

Having taught in film schools since 1976, I am continually impressed by the high level of visual competence of the students on the one hand, and their complete lack of preparation for achieving viability in the business on the other.

Many wish to enter the film and video world, few survive. This is not because these worlds are crueler or less forgiving than other business fields, but because the high costs and uncertain returns have tended to concentrate the power in major companies. Now the explosion of new viewing technologies, and their high economic potential, has opened up the area to those entrepreneurial producers who are willing to become trained in the history, aesthetics and craft of the industry. The creative and business-wise producer has never had a better chance to flourish.

But prosperity does not come from high purpose alone. One's goals and purposes must be supported by an active professional understanding of the rules the other players live by. You do not have to agree with these rules, but you must know them.

RECOMMENDED BOOKS ON FILM

GENERAL FILMMAKING
DIRECTING THE FILM; Sherman; Acrobat, 1988
FRAME BY FRAME; Sherman; Acrobat, 1986
INDEPENDENT FEATURE FILM PRODUCTION;
    Goodell; St. Martin's, 1982

THE BUSINESS
INDECENT EXPOSURE; McClintick; Morrow, 1982
FINAL CUT; Bach; Plume, 1985
ADVENTURES IN THE SCREEN TRADE; Goldman;
    Warner, 1983
DARK VICTORY; Moldea; Viking, 1986
REEL POWER; Litwak; Morrow, 1986
PRODUCING, FINANCING AND DISTRIBUTING FILM:
    A Comprehensive Legal and Business Guide;
    Baumgarten, Farber and Fleisher; Limelight, 1990
POSITIONING: The Battle for Your Mind; Trout & Ries;
    McGraw Hill, 1981

SCREENWRITING
SCREENPLAY; Field; Dell, 1979
THE SCREENWRITER'S WORKBOOK; Field; Dell, 1984

ESSAYS
AMERICAN CINEMA; Sarris; University of Chicago, 1985
HITCHCOCK'S FILMS; Wood; A.S. Barnes, 1969
WHAT IS CINEMA?—Vols 1 and 2; Bazin, Univ. of
    California Press, 1967, 1971

OTHER CRAFT BOOKS
BROOKS STANDARD RATE BOOKS—annual updates
FILM SCHEDULING; Singleton, 1984
FILM SCHEDULING/FILM BUDGETING WORKBOOK;
    Singleton, 1984
MOVIE PRODUCTION AND BUDGET FORMS . . .
    INSTANTLY; Singleton, 1985

JOURNALS
Daily Variety
Variety
Film Comment
American Film
Boxoffice
American Cinematographer
Knowledge Industry publications

INDEX

NOTES

NOTES

NOTES

NOTES

NOTES